Table of Contents

Introduction 1

Chapter 1: How To Be Happy 4

Chapter 2: How To Do Away With Negativity 16

Chapter 3: How To Believe In Yourself 27

Chapter 4: How To Live In Higher Awareness or Higher Vibration 41

Chapter 5: Core Beliefs In Yourself 49

Chapter 6: Ways To Harness Positive Energy 63

Chapter 7: The Key To Happiness 72

Chapter 8: Healing Past Traumas And Fears 83

Chapter 9: Happiness and Morality: 101

Chapter 10: How To Boost Your Happiness 108

Chapter 11: Workbook Section and Journaling 116

INTRODUCTION

Are you happy with each and every moment in your life and with your day-to-day living? Or do you find yourself in various states of confusion, bleakness, anxiety or other negative factors or qualities that tend to affect your day in a manner that isn't so positive? How To Be Happy and Stay That Way, will give you unlimited tips and tricks on how to be a happier person and how to be a good positive person and how to hone in on living this way on a day to day basis. This book will allow you to become the powerhouse of positivity that you were truly meant to be and let you focus in on all your blessed and wonderful qualities that you may have not even knew existed. Let this book be your resource for being a happy and good person and let you be the real you and the happier you that you were always meant to be! Cheers!

We all strive to be happy and to be fulfilled in huge ways in life. What is the concept of happiness and why do so many of us seek to find it? You might ask yourself this question many times throughout your existence. What is the notion of happiness and what does it all mean? Well happiness is really the key to existing in a very positive state of mind in the world and it's something most people feel they want to experience but many haven't fully experienced or grasped it. In this book, you'll learn the many various facets of what it means to be a happy person and the different paths it takes to lead to being a happier and more fulfilled human being.

Happiness isn't material or worldly gains. It isn't a Ferrari that you buy on a whim though of course, that can lead to happiness in some form. Happiness of course, is simply a state of mind. Happiness is a harmonious wondrous mental state that one can attain to striving towards and being at once you've dealt with all the obstacles that are there to stop you from reaching this amazing state of mind.

Have you ever wondered what it was like to truly be happy and to truly be in a state of extreme bliss and that feeling of ecstasy and all the wonderful associations that come from feeling what it's like to be this way? Well, if you have look no further- you'll find the key steps it takes to getting to that place of love and light and bliss, harmony and the place you've always wanted to be. Happiness can be accessed to you at any time for you have the power within you to grasp it whenever you need it.

One way of achieving true happiness is through the power of positivity and goodness and this is only one of the few methods you can use to get to this blissful and grand state of mind. If you really want to feel good about yourself and your life, then you will want to take each and every lesson in this book that will assist you in becoming a more fulfilled and more successful and happier you! If you have any form of depression, there are tips as well on how to successfully handle or deal with depression in any form through natural means and achieve a better and more blissful inner person which is what you were truly meant to be, rather than someone who might feel negative in any form or might be prone to any kind of depressive issues.

If you truly want to be happy, you'll have to learn how to discover the true goodness within you, and all of its elements and glory. You'll need to bask in what is the true goodness within yourself and all of these elements and focus on the beautiful and wonderful qualities that you do have that will allow you to appreciate the person that you truly are and who you were meant to be.

Chapter 1

HOW TO BE HAPPY

Do you feel as if you're a happy person in life or do you feel as if things just aren't as great for you as they used to be? It's hard to define what happiness truly is. It's something that we feel somewhere deep within but it's also something that is a greater part of ourselves. We may not really be sure exactly what true happiness is, or most people may not understand what that means. There are many ways of finding happiness and there are many complex definitions for what happiness truly is. Do you feel as if you want more out of life? Does it feel as if you're just not doing as good as you thought you would do or that you're not succeeding or achieving the great things that you want to achieve in life?

This book can help you understand the key elements to being a happier person, and how to improve your life and your lifestyle, and turn it around and turn it into something that is going to be extremely beneficial and positive for you, because the truth is that you deserve the very best in life and you deserve to be happy and you deserve everything that life has to offer. You don't deserve to be in a place of negativity, confusion, or anxiety or fear. Those are the emotions we want to stray away from. We want to go towards the emotions of love, light, happiness, and joy and peace, and those emotions are the ones that will allow us to harness the concept of positivity, happiness, and gear more towards being a happier, healthier and whole you.

Happiness is not an easy feat to achieve or attain. Many people in life yearn to know what it feels like to truly be happy. It's definitely not something that is always easy to be able to feel achieve. Why do so many people desire the concept of happiness? It's because, most people are at the very opposite of this state. Most people are in a state of depression, anger, angst, confusion, misery and many of those other states of mind that are extremely unhealthy and negative. Being happy isn't just a state of mind or a positive mentality-it's an amazing feeling and lifestyle that someone can have once they achieve that very positive and blissful mindset and way of thinking and living.

What is happiness? Most people can't even grasp the concept of what true happiness is or what the ideation really means. They only know and feel what they perceive true happiness is. Happiness is one of the few concepts that we can only begin to imagine and peel away the many varying layers of. We are all human beings living the ways of the world in our own ideations and means, however, we all strive to be happy decent good people in our own ways.

Happiness is an emotional state characterized by feelings of joy, contentment, and satisfaction. It is often associated with positive experiences, a sense of well-being, and a general positive outlook on life. Happiness can be influenced by various factors, including personal circumstances, relationships, health and individual perspectives.

It's important to focus on being happy and being good positive healthy people. Happiness is the true bliss that many people just can't seem to fully comprehend. Happiness is bliss and a state of mind of being in utter peace with yourself and your life, and just being elated at many things that happen in life and it's an amazing great state of mind and place to be in! True nirvana comes with great experience and practice and it's not always something that can be achieved.

Happiness is a wonderful place that most people strive to be in, yet can't always find the understanding and meaning of or the means to get to or feel. You might feel happiness sometimes or feel twinges of happiness, yet to truly be happy is something that most people just haven't truly experienced or know of. In order to be happy, you must first understand that it's important to have an extremely positive state of mind. Without having a positive state of mind or living in a state of goodness and positivity, you truly can't be happy or possess the notion of happiness. The definition of happiness is showing the pleasure of contentment in something. In order to be happy, we must first possess the concept of love and goodness and be in a constant state of positivity.

Being in a state of positivity and love is not an easy thing to do. Not many people can understand or grasp that concept or have even heard of it. The base for happiness is love and light and it's extremely important to harness this base of love in order to achieve true inner happiness, love light and bliss. True inner happiness is love, light and bliss energy and true light. This is what it truly means to be a happy person.

The basis for happiness is love and light, so it is extremely important that in order to achieve true inner happiness and goodness, you must focus on being love and light. Now what exactly does this mean? In order to be love and light, you must always be in a state of harmony and goodness and want good for others, and be in a state of being extremely positive and a positive good person and build from there on. You will have to start off small and begin building the concept from there. Being in a state of love just means that you are of love and goodness and love every person and everything that is good and decent and have a higher idea of love in mind when it comes to each and every living being that graces your presence.

For many people, achieving that concept of being true love and light within yourself means that a person has had to undergo some form of spiritual awakening or enlightenment, or awakening of a higher awareness. Not every person has to undergo this, but for many that is where this concept of love or light does come from. Others just feel this way in general but in order to attain true happiness it's extremely important that you feel happiness, goodness and bliss energy throughout your life and within your entire body. You can even do this by doing breathing exercises which help raise your vibration, or just by thinking happy and great amazing positive thoughts.

Some thoughts you can have in order to raise your vibration and focus on being a happier more positive person are

I am beautiful

I am a blessed gracious human being

I am love light and abundance

I love myself unconditionally

I focus on that which is positive and harmonious

I only want that which is beneficial for me and for others

I am a wonderful caring kind good person

I possess great capabilities and strengths

I am a wonderful, caring kind special person

I am one of the best humans to exist out there

It's very important that you also focus on being positive and having positive affirmations in your life. You can write out affirmations of your own or purchase books for this resource. Thinking positive, beautiful thoughts out loud, reading them out loud or in your mind can have really beneficial effects on your state of mind and thinking and can and will build the foundation for creating a love-based happy state of mind and way of thinking and will assist you in being a truly happy person that is full of love, light, beauty and positivity.

So again, the key to being happy is by building a foundation of love, light goodness, and positive thoughts and a great positive state of mind. This is one of the few ways and keys of achieving true happiness, enlightenment and allowing you to experience true bliss, harmony and beauty within your life. True happiness is allowing you to see, experience and perceive the beauty within each and every thing that you do and allow you to focus on that beauty, bask in it and be an incredibly happy person as a result of it. True happiness is an amazing bliss, energy and bliss that a person feels deep within and within their souls and self. It's a love for everything and everyone around them and an appreciation for life and to be love and to love everything that is, rather than focus on negativity or hate or be that which is hateful or harmful.

Being happy is a blissful and elated state of mind. Many people think that being happy is actually many other concepts and ideas, or people might not have much of a clue as to what true happiness is, or they haven't yet experienced or grasped the true nature of it. There are varying levels of happiness out there as well, once you finally do attain that true happiness that exists. There is the concept of true enlightenment and bliss happiness which is the ultimate level of nirvana and something that is talked about in religions like Buddhism and to achieve that level of happiness is something that can't be described. That is in fact the highest level of happiness and there are also varying levels within that genre of being and feeling true happiness. Now what is enlightenment? Enlightenment is the concept of achieving a gracious higher awareness and it's one of the highest levels of spiritual awakening or achieving one of the highest levels of spiritual awakening. There are levels beneath this idea of true happiness or enlightenment and there are probably about several levels of happiness that a person can truly experience.

There are other levels of happiness, and a person doesn't necessarily have to attain a level of enlightenment or nirvana in order to reach any form of true happiness, however the concept stays the same. The level of bliss is just going to be lesser than with those who have achieved a level of enlightenment. The bliss level for those who've attained enlightenment are extreme levels of bliss and happiness and light energy. For those who simply want to be happier or happy people, it's namely and mostly about practicing and thinking these positive thoughts and ideas and achieving a happier more positive state of mind in order to achieve that overall level of true happiness. It's also about having an extremely positive state of mind by thinking powerful positive thoughts that will take over and change your way of thinking and elevate your day-to-day life in a huge and beneficial way.

Being happy is a total state of mind and a lifestyle and life changing way of being that you will want to obtain and live through no matter what the situation is. Happiness is the beauty, wonder love and key to living a fulfilling and healthy beautiful and grand life as opposed to not being this way and being the opposite of it.

Happiness is the only way of life, the truth and the love and bliss you'll seek to obtain and find and once you do, you will never be the same. Being a happy person is one of the few wonderful ways of living a gracious beautiful life with goodness, love, and light present in it. It may not be easy to achieve a total state of happiness, but there are states of happiness you can obtain that allow you to be a happy person in general and let you live a more fulfilled, and blessed life.

We are all souled beings on this planet experiencing it through our own lens and the only true and real lens to experience our beautiful, amazing lives is through the power of happiness. Being happy doesn't always have to be a state of mind exclusively, for it can also be defined through bursts of experiences, that allow this level of goodness to come forth and you can still experience happiness in all kinds of ways without having to be a total state of complete goodness which is energetic bliss and happiness somewhere within you.

Sunshine and rainbows is truly what happiness can be. It really is the sunshine that we bask in and the beauty of nature and rainbows and everything that is natural and wonderful. Nature is one of the few ways a person can reach greater states of happiness and positivity so definitely seek nature as a wonderful, and special way of achieving any fom of bliss or goodness. It is also a beautiful, amazing bliss energy and the realization that each and everything we do on this planet relates to the beauty of love, life, and nature and the world.

One way of achieving happiness or one concept of being happy is the true appreciation of love and nature and all that encompasses the beauty of the planet and the world.

The foundation for happiness is a bliss energy that we're seeking to obtain. This is the powerhouse that we're wanting to build upon. Now it doesn't always have to be an energy, it can be a strong feeling or a feeling within us or a belief however it is rooted in a beautiful, wonderful energy.

Nature is the beauty of what has been created on this planet by the Creator, also the appreciation of that which is the planet and of creation itself. To love and appreciate and enjoy each and every amazing living creation is one by product of true happiness and is happiness thus forth.

Now, we are the keys to our own happiness. The key to happiness is actually our own selves, and that's another way. We can actually access our own souls, and the loving light that is within us, and that is through our own selves in our own souls, and this is another way that we can build on the positivity through the beauty of our souls, because the soul is the key to our eternal selves.

We are the beauty and light that we seek. We actually possess this amazing beauty and light within ourselves, and we are the key to our own happiness. We are beauty love, light, wonder in amazement, and we are the ones that possess the keys to our own happiness, and to unlimited happiness and elevated states of happiness, where we can actually build on what we actually possessed, or do possess when it comes to the concept of happiness.

Love is the epitome of happiness, beauty and tremendous blessings in our world and life.

The truth about happiness

The truth about happiness is that it is something that can easily be achieved or attained by a little understanding and practice, and it is something that many people can grow to obtain and become a part of. Happiness is a beautiful, wonderful facet that anybody can grasp and become a part of, if they understand the very core of this subject and what real true happiness consists of.

Positive therapists and psychotherapists define the concept of happiness as a feeling of excitement or ecstasy or comfort that can be readily or easily accessed at any given point. They feel as if in order to live a happy or fulfilling life, you'll need to fill it with extremely positive and fulfilling activities, but especially positive ones. Positive psychology focuses on your strengths and virtues and not on your fears or other negative aspects.

Happiness is an experience that can vary from person to person. It is often a combination of positive emotions, life satisfaction, and a wonderful sense of purpose and fulfillment. There are ways a person can contribute to a greater sense of happiness and those things include positive relationships, practicing gratitude, engaging in meaningful activities, taking care of physical and mental health, and finding a greater sense of purpose. What brings happiness to a person can definitely vary from person to person as well.

Chapter 2

How To Do Away With Negativity

Positivity is one of the few aspects or areas of life that many people may find hard to reach. It may seem incredibly difficult to be a positive happy person and to focus on those aspects of life that are positive in nature. It may seem to make more sense to gravitate towards that which is negative in nature or that which seems to be on the downside. The reason for this is because many people are in depressed states in their life, and they are not the person they once were or used to be. Traumas, imbalances, and other life issues may have affected or taken over them and they may not be the person they once were, or the happy person they remember.

The problem with this way of thinking is that it doesn't help a person live their life or accomplish the things they want in life, or allows them to further move forward in life or attain any form of success. In order to be successful in life, you'll need to do away with negativity and gravitate towards an extremely positive state of mind. In order to further oneself in life, or even just be a happy normal person, a person needs to have a completely positive state of mind. The only way to cultivate a positive state of mind is to do away with all the negatives in your life. It's important to focus on the positive aspects in your life and to stop focusing on the negative things.

The gateway to happiness, peace, bliss, and beauty is actually an incredibly positive state of mind. It's extremely important for us to focus on being positive people, because that is what is going to turn us into happy, healthy, and fully fulfilled human beings. Now we might not fully understand what that means. You might think that there are other ways to achieve happiness and there really is I mean you can access being happy at any time you can be a happy person, but if you want to find true happiness and truly, but just going to eradicate any of those negative feelings, that you have feelings of hate, fear, doubt, self-doubt, self-destruction, confusion, anxiety, or angst, then you really want to focus on being an extremely positive person and focus on those positive feelings that you have somewhere deep down within you, you can do this by saying positive things, and repeating mantras and positive affirmations.

It's extremely important to focus on doing away with any negative thoughts or feelings you might have somewhere within you. You can do so by practicing this every time you find yourself having a negative thought or feeling, it's important that you focus on positive thoughts, and replace each and every negative thoughts or way of thinking with a positive mantra, affirmation, thought or statement.

How on earth can a person do away with or get rid of any form of negativity out there?

Negativity tends to breed more negativity unfortunately, and it's very important that you build upon positive beliefs and actions only. It's a very important thing that you focus on the positive aspects of your life only and steer clear of any negative and confusing aspects or anything that may cause you stress or anxiety.

Are you a negative or positive person?

Getting rid of negativity is not as easy as it sounds since most people tend to focus on exactly that. For example, when you wake up in the morning, do you focus on how happy you feel, and are you excited to start the day? Or do you usually feel groggy and upset and think "oh boy, I have another horrible day to deal with" or something of that nature?

Many people tend to think exactly that- they think "oh great, another day for me" or "Oh No, I have to wake up and go to my horrible job and deal with work." When you wake up in the morning- what exactly are you thinking? In order to help yourself be a happy person you'll have to do away with each and every negative thought you have and learn to focus on a positive mindset. It may not be that easy for you to do if you tend to think in a negative manner. It may sound like an easy and simple concept, but for many it's not as easy as it sounds.

If you're a pretty positive person then of course you'll think in a more positive mindset, but that doesn't necessarily mean that you're going to have a completely positive state of mind. You might be an optimistic person and think more on the bright side, but you may have doubts and fears here and there and in general. Being a positive person is a great quality to have and it's something that might help you succeed and do well in life, however, you may still be missing out on many important elements and successes in life if you don't have a completely positive state of mind. You're most likely missing out on many amazing moments that you could be having in life, and the ultimate bliss and happiness that comes with having a completely amazing optimistic state of mind and living in that moment of happiness and love, light and true bliss.

What is living in the moment?

You may have heard of the concept of "living in the moment," but what exactly is This Idea, concept, and term and what does it mean. Also how does it relate to me and my life and achieving an incredibly positive beautiful state of mind and how can I use it to my advantage? Living in the moment is the concept of basically enjoying the moment in a hugely blissful amazing, wonderful way, or enjoying each and every moment in your life in this particular way, however having a positive state of mind is the one way you can elevate this concept of living in the moment. For example, let's say you have a lunch break at work. Well living in the moment is basking in your lunch break, and just being happy which most people do, but sometimes that happiness or those moments or feelings are just increased in some form.

In order to be incredibly positive, you first have to grasp the concept of living in The moment and exactly what it means and use it to apply to your life in each and every moment you exist. As a beginner learning these concepts though, you don't have to apply the concept to every moment- it can actually be applied and used to specific moments throughout the day in order to elevate your positivity and happiness.

In order to focus on living in the moment and to begin to apply this idea to your life, you'll need to just remind yourself to do it throughout the day. Imagine yourself waking up, and you feel happy enough that you're getting up and starting the day. Do you focus on each moment, or do you just rush through the process? When you live in the moment, you take specific moments and really bask in the happiness you might feel. Maybe dressing and rushing to get to work isn't the best time to try to focus on living in the moment, however, you can do that on your drive to work. If you drive to work, what you'll need to do is really focus on the positive aspect of the drive rather than thinking about nothing important, worrying about minor things in your life, or just kind of listening to music or doing the usual that you do.

If you're listening to music, you'll want to really hone in and focus on the beauty and positive nature of the song or music. If you're just driving and thinking about nothing, you will need to focus on the beauty of the song and how happy it makes you or how it elevates your mood. That's what living in the moment is- it's enjoying each and every moment you can throughout the day and throughout your life, and loving the happiness and enjoyment you get out of these particular moments or activities.

If you work from home, the second you get up, you can focus on the happiness and goodness you feel that you're working from home and how much easier your life is that you don't have to drive to a job- which is usually how many people tend to feel about this particular lifestyle. But you'll want to really bask in the glory of happiness you feel about being able to enjoy getting up and going right to work and not having to worry about gas, the headache of driving etc.

You can truly bask in the breakfast you're eating or the coffee you're drinking and just enjoy the moments, however you'll need to do that in a more elevated way in order to really live in the situation and elevate it's presence and beauty in your life and allow it to affect your life in an even more positive way. You can allow this feeling of living in the moment to sky ball and become more positive and allow the energy to get better and better. You can access your happiness by living in the moment during different times of the day and elevate your happiness and energy during those times and enjoy those moments more than others.

Are you a negative person?

If you're a negative person, then your situation might be a little different than the person who thinks extremely positively or in a positive manner. Do you usually think in tones of negativity or think "oh gosh, this is happening to me right now." Do you tend to focus on the negative things that happen to you in life, or are you usually depressed or feeling down most of the time. If so, then you're probably more of a negative person and you're definitely in a greater need of having to focus on the positive aspects of your life or life in general. You definitely will need a boost of ideas on how to think positively and how to use those concepts to change your way of thinking and change your entire life and be a happier or happy person in general.

If you're a negative person in general or tend to focus on the down things in life, then this book really can and will help change your perspective on things in life, and it will even allow you to change your mindset and way of thinking and allow you to become an incredibly happy and positive person. You will learn how to turn all those negative ideations and thoughts into positive ones, and those ideas will allow you to snowball those positive effects and be a much happier, healthier person and even be the happiest best person you can be and what you set out to do!

If you're more of a negative person or think with negative thoughts that's totally ok! Many people tend to think the same way. They just think their lives are boring and mundane. They may be unhappy with their current state in life that they're in, or they're seeking or searching for something more out there. It's completely ok to feel this way simply because it's not your fault you feel this way and even if it is- that state of mind can easily be changed with a little bit of practice and the amazing magic of positive thinking. You can be a happier, healthier, brighter, and more amazing person than you were before. You can also be the person you once were before these negative changes took place! You too can be like those positive people you see out there who seem to be much happier than you. The secret also is, many of those people who seem positive and happy probably have their own issues too or are living in state of unawareness and they lack the true concept of positivity and happiness, that you think they might possess.

Being a negative person is not always the worst type of situation to be in. It can be of great benefit for you to learn how to be positive and learn how to challenge yourself by being the optimistic person you're truly meant to be, rather than the person you are. You can easily turn negative thoughts into incredibly beneficial ones by substituting negative thoughts for positive ones. Throughout the day, every time you harness a negative thought, just replace it with a positive one and that's basically it. Once you begin doing this regularly, then you'll slowly re-train your mind and rewire your mind into becoming an incredibly hopeful powerhouse, and you will start to think in a more positive manner, and your life will begin to change.

There are several techniques that someone can use for challenging or eradicating negative thoughts. These include

1. Cognitive restructuring which Is identifying and challenging negative or irrational thoughts by examining anything that might be supporting or contradicting them.
2. Thought-stopping, which is interrupting negative thoughts by mentally saying stop and replacing them with more positive or realistic decent thoughts.
3. Reframing is looking for alternative perspectives or interpretations of a situation that could be more balanced or positive.
4. Evidence gathering- which is collecting evidence that supports or contradicts negative thoughts to gain a more accurate or balanced perspective.
5. There is also mindfulness which is the practice of observing and accepting negative thoughts without judgment, and allowing them to simply just pass without becoming too worried about their effects.

6. Labeling: When a negative thought comes about, label it as a 'thought' or story rather than an absolute truth which helps to create distance and lessen its impact.
7. Observe the thoughts: This is just observing negative thoughts as passing mental events without worrying too much about what they really mean.
8. Grounding: this is bringing attention to the thought at hand by focusing on your senses, especially the feeling of your feet on the ground or the sounds around you, to shift attention away from any kind of negative thoughts.

Chapter 3

How To Believe In Yourself

You Can Accomplish Almost Anything You Want if you Truly Desire

Believing in your gifts, talents and yourself is not always an easy feat to accomplish. Do you often find yourself doubting your abilities, or wondering if you're good enough to do a certain or specific task? Don't worry- you're definitely not the only one. Statistics show that 85% percent of people actually doubt themselves or their specific abilities and what they're actually able to accomplish. Accomplishing things can be a challenging and fearful feat to do anyway. People often wonder whether they'll be able to do the task at hand, or whether they'll fail or be rejected.

Most people tend to focus on the negatives rather than the positives and let their fears take over them. This is a completely normal way to think and feel as a person really isn't sure whether they'll be able to do something whether it's taking up a sport, a board game, or any kind of hobby or task or even a job. There is a secret however when it comes to believing in yourself and any task at hand. The truth is that many people have many hidden talents and abilities and might even be able to accomplish and do things they really aren't able to. Many people might doubt themselves from the start and wonder whether they're able to accomplish anything. Many people tend to fear rejection and that is a huge problem when it comes to believing in a person's self and believing in your own personal abilities and gifts.

Since most people can truly almost do most things, they put their mind to, that's one positive idea that can help a person believe in their own selves. This is of course a special secret that not every person has discovered. That's because many people live mundane lives, or stay in the same fields, the same jobs they've always stayed in, and tend to steer towards the same things they've always done. People rarely change it up, or do anything different and if they do, they don't come to the realization of what they're truly able to accomplish. Never shortchange yourself or feel that you're not good enough to do something. The truth is, you're the only one who can do and set out to do what you need to accomplish and what you need to do in life. You're the only one you are challenging. There's no one else around, it's only you and yourself. You can basically do just about anything you put your mind to most of the time.

That's because the human being possesses a brain and mind that is highly gifted and unique, and you actually have the capability of doing and accomplishing feats you actually didn't think you could ever do. You as a human being possess the capability that no other creature does. You can think, speak, talk, and actually communicate differently from other animals and that is actually an amazing and great quality to possess. That's definitely one place to start- to focus on the great qualities you do have as a human being with the great mind you do possess. Other animals do possess great minds just like you, and they have other qualities you as a human may not have, but they lack the ability to communicate the way a human can which involves writing, reading and other methods of communication. You as a human actually harness the gifts that you need in order to do anything you really put your mind to and that is an important truth to know.

It's important to believe in yourself as a person simply because no one else will. Your friends and family may believe in you as a person or in your gifts or abilities and talents, but they're not you and they're not the ones attempting to accomplish the very tasks you're trying to accomplish- whether it's having a more positive state of mind, or trying to get a better job or just achieve greater success in life. You may have a hoard of followers on TikTok or Instagram, or family and friends who support anything you do, or you may not have much support. They aren't the ones who are attempting to do the things you are, so even they believe in you, you may find yourself doubt you and the things you're able to do.

In order to believe in yourself, your talents and hidden gifts, you'll need to focus on the positive and beneficial things you've done in your life and the things you have accomplished. Are you good at a particular sport? Did you achieve anything in grade school or high school? Are you really good at your particular job? Did you discover at some point that you were good at something and somehow you could make a lot of money doing it? Are you a cashier at a store and just good at dealing with people and friendly and outgoing? Anything you do in life, can allow you to believe in yourself and your gifts and talents. Now what is a hidden gift?

When I say hidden gift, I just mean everyone has hidden gifts and talents and important things they are actually really good at or can be great at, but haven't truly discovered yet. That is again because with the human brain and mind, you're actually able to accomplish a lot more than you think or understand. Have you always wanted to be a good chess player but just felt you weren't able to do it or that you couldn't understand the game? Have you always wanted to write but felt you were unable to do it? There's a secret that Is waiting for you to unleash- and that is that you're actually able to accomplish any of these things with your hidden talents and amazing gifts that only you as a person possess due to the many amazing capabilities you possess as a human being.

You might think "I could never play chess. "I could never write an article, or be a great baseball player." The truth is, you can actually do any of these things if you truly want to. Sometimes with sports, it's not always simple due to the fact that there might be limited capabilities someone possesses, or due to the difficulty of what is involved but that doesn't mean that somewhere deep within you, you're not able accomplish that feat if you didn't practice hard enough or try. The most important aspect that you'll really need to know is that, YOU truly have the capability and possess the nature of doing most or anything you truly want to do.

That of course is the most important aspect to grasp of this lesson. The fact that you have hidden talents and abilities that you're completely unaware of, should help you as a person understand that you should believe in yourself when it applies to anything that you need to do in life. It's also extremely important to focus on the positive aspects that you possess and to build on those positives, so that you're a powerhouse of positivity rather than anything negative or anything that might contribute to thinking in a negative form or manner. You can do anything you put your mind to that is simply because, as a human being you possess a great mind and great abilities that are capable of great and amazing achievements.

Believing in yourself can involve creating self-confidence and there are ways to create a more positive self-image.

1. Recognize your strengths: Reflect on your past achievements or any goals you have accomplished. It's important to acknowledge your abilities and the really great special qualities that you do possess
2. Challenge any form of self-doubt: identify and challenge any kind of negativity or negative self-talk or any beliefs that limit your confidence. You'll need to replace them with very positive and empowering thoughts which will boost your confidence and give you a more positive outlook on yourself

3. Set realistic goals: Set goals that align with your passions and values. Break your goals down into smaller, manageable steps to build confidence as you progress into the greater brighter better you that you deserve to be!
4. Surround yourself with positive people who support you: Seek out positive support and relationships. Surround yourself with people who support and believe in you and you will boost your self-esteem and your happiness overall.

Building self-belief can take time and effort. You'll need to be very patient with yourself and practice self-compassion as you work on building a greater belief in yourself and your abilities. Just remember, you can accomplish and be and do anything you want in your world, reality, and life and there is no one that can stop you from doing these things or bring you down.

How to be Confident:

It's extremely important to focus on being confident and believing in each and anything you ever do in your life- of course as long as it's positive and beneficial to others and not of any harm or wrongdoing. That's because anything that isn't positive or beneficial to others is something that isn't part of being a positive good person and being optimistic in general. Being confident in yourself isn't always an easy task. That's simply because you're not really sure if you're able to believe in yourself as a person or feel as if you're just good enough to do many different things. There are many people who are incredibly confident, and there are others who may not feel this way at all.

Not everyone is going to believe in their own strengths or gifts, and that's alright for you to feel this way. If you're a confident person, then you probably don't have any issues with feeling positive about your abilities and the things you're able to do in life. You can snowball the effects of how you feel by focusing on your positive qualities and aspects and allowing them to assist you with greater feelings of being able to do the things you need to do in life. If you lack confidence, then you're definitely in need of understanding that you're actually an incredibly powerful person who can do just about anything you put your mind to or anything you truly desire.

In order to focus on your talents and strengths you'll need to go back to the greater understanding that you're not exactly who you think you are. You actually have a plethora of hidden abilities and talents that you as a person are unaware of. That's one important piece of the puzzle that will help you build your self-esteem and understand assist you with gaining a greater understanding of yourself and what you're able to accomplish as a human being. Maybe you wanted to run a marathon, but it seemed too impossible for you.

Maybe you just wanted to be a runner but felt as if you were unable to do it. The hidden truth is, if you truly desire, you're able to do any of these things, and maybe you feel you can't run an entire marathon- you can always run three miles, five miles, or do whatever mileage you feel comfortable with. Any of those tasks are a huge accomplishment for any person. The truth of the scenario is, if millions of people can run a marathon- why can't you? There are also disabled people who run marathons and people with limited physical capabilities who do amazing things. If they're able to do these things then why can't a person with full physical capabilities? If you feel that you're just unable to do specific things in life or tasks, just think of the fact that people with limited abilities and limited physical capacity are able to accomplish these things, so why can't you?

There are several very effective techniques that a person can do to build their self-confidence.

1. Positive self-talk: it's important to replace self-critical or negative thoughts with positive and very encouraging ones. You should constantly remind yourself of your strengths and any of your successful feats in life.
2. Set achievable goals: You'll need to break down larger goals into smaller steps which will allow or help you to boost your confidence and motivation.

3. Celebrate your achievements: Acknowledge and celebrate your accomplishments. This aids with building a much greater self-image and confidence as well
4. Practice self-care: Take care of your physical and mental self and and engage in activities that help boost you and make you feel good such as exercise, sleep relaxation, massage, acupuncture etc.
5. Face your fears: it's important to gradually overcome and confront your fears and challenges. Each time you do this you can boost your self-esteem and confidence.
6. Surround yourself with positive support and groups who will aid you: Surround yourself with mentors, friedns, and people who lift you up and support you and seek out support groups that encourage you to grow and assist you with your true potential.

It's extremely important to focus on the positive capabilities you do have in order to be confident in yourself, and also to understand that you are a quality and important person on this planet and that you should love yourself unconditionally.

Fearing rejection

Fearing rejection is one of the few notions that many people tend to feel when they undertake or undergo a particular task, or is a way of thinking that many people tend to have in life. People fear rejection in all kinds of ways however, you don't need to live like this or think like this any longer! Fearing rejection is an unfortunate way of thinking that many adults and humans have in today's society and it's one negative quality that needs to be addressed when it dealing with trying to do away with a negative state of mind and getting back to a more positive one.

Fearing rejection is a huge issue amongst people in general. People often feel as if any task they undergo they may fail at or end up not doing well at. People tend to fear all forms of rejection or failure. This is a huge problem for most people for it stops people from being able to partake in specific activities in life, and stops people from being able to reach their goals and allows them to mostly just stay stuck in the current situations they're in.

You as a person should have more confidence within yourself and not allow your fears to take over your actions or allow you to let your fear of rejection dictate what steps or actions you need to take in your life. Fear of rejection is an irrational belief that many people hold when it comes to undertaking many tasks or goals in life and it needs to be eliminated overall.

No one should undergo tasks in their daily life or want to accomplish goals yet fear failure and then never even try for this is what happens to many people. They seek to accomplish things in life, yet their fear of rejection or failure is so strong, they'd rather not even attempt to try for those goals or actions and just stay in the same place they are at.

People should freely undergo tasks or attempt to accomplish their goals without any fear or care for how the results will turn out. In order to overcome your fear of failure or rejection, you'll need to undergo tasks and goals with total confidence and positivity and know that no matter what you do, you will still be a success and that there is no reason to fear achieving that goal or trying to simply because at least you tried if that's the worst case scenario.

You should raise your confidence levels and freely be open to completing your goals and tasks without the fear of rejection. It's ok to attempt to undergo tasks and goals and not be successful at them- this is something that does happen with many people or most. It's okay to be rejected or not do well or even fail for at least you tried. The most surprising, amazing thing is that you more than likely aren't going to fail at all, yet you thjnk you will.

This is one of the more surprising findings you will discover. The task or goal you feel you won't do good in, is probably the field in which you need to be or the task you must partake in, in order to progress in your life and in order to move forward and evolve as a person and as a talented successful human being.

Fearing rejection is a waste of time in your life and it will get you nowhere. If you live in constant fear, then you will have a hard time developing yourself as a person and taking on your tasks and goals that will help you evolve and develop your own self, your personality, your gifts, your talents, and who you are. Living in fear is something we should try to eliminate or do away with in order to progress in life and become more successful in anything that we do or attempt to accomplish.

You need to learn to live through the lens of positivity and through the lens of beauty, love and light and not through the notions of fear or negativity. If you live through the lens of positivity and not through fear or anything negative and it'll be much easier for you to accomplish your goals in your task and deeds, and all the great things that you want to do. You will find it much easier to accomplish and do these things. If you live through fear and the fear base ideation, such as anxiety, rejection, failure, and any negative notions, then you will have a very hard time accomplishing all the things that you want to accomplish. Ways to deal with fearing rejection involve reminding yourself of your worth, keep things in perspective, face your fears and deal with it, reject negative self-talk, figure out what scares you about the rejection, lean on your support network, and talk to a professional.

A fear of rejection can have a huge impact in people's lives. People are terrified of failing at tasks they have to do or taking on big projects or attempting to achieve things they've never attempted before due to the difficult nature of them sometimes. However, it's important that we focus on living with love, light, and positivity and eliminating any fears that we may hold about anything and realizing our own capabilities, and that we're able to do just about anything we set out to do, intend to do and put our mind to.

Chapter 4

How To Live In Higher Awareness or Higher Vibration

What is living in awareness and light?

The idea of living in awareness is the concept of having a higher awareness of life, reality and the current state we're in and the life that we're living. It's extremely important that we're not living in a state of hormones, and a lack of understanding of life and humanity which is how most people tend to live their lives or how they grasp reality. We need to live in a higher state of mind that isn't of the lower vibration and the lesser animalistic ways of thinking. What are the animalistic ways of thinking- these ways of thinking are fear, rage, aggression, sexual hunger and desire, lack of confidence, lack of interest in life etc. It's extremely important to understand that you as a human or we as humans need to live in a higher more civilized state which involves a greater state of awareness and understanding of anything around you or that which is happening to us.

Awareness is the state of being conscious or cognizant of something such as your surroundings, thoughts, emotions or the existence of something. It involves being attentive and perceptive. A higher awareness refers to an expanded state of consciousness or perception that goes beyond our everyday experiences and allows for a deeper understanding of ourselves, others and the world surrounding us. It involves mindfulness, intuition, insight and spirituality.

Most people tend to live their lives in a very monotonous nature without thinking of the things they're actually doing or having any level of awareness of the actions they're undergoing or doing. People generally live their lives in a very robotic nature and without a general awareness or understanding of many concepts in life. People just 'live' and they aren't aware of their actions, thoughts or the feelings they're even having and it's not always an easy concept to actually possess a higher awareness of actions that happen in life. It's extremely important to live in a higher state of consciousness and a higher vibration as well.

Now what is a higher vibration? A higher vibration is a vibration of one's frequency or energy and it's important that our energy is of the highest vibration and that we focus on raising it so that we are of goodness, positivity, oneness and light. It's very important that we live in a state of oneness and bliss and focus on positive, pure, and good thoughts that actually assist us in gaining that connection we have to a much higher positive and blissful vibration, rather than that of a lower fear based dark or negative vibration.

When someone Is of a lower vibration or living in a lower vibration, they are in fact living in a state of disharmony, disillusionment and living in a more fear-based reality which involves the negative aspects of fear, hate, anger, aggression and many other aspects that aren't of a positive quality. When we focus on raising our vibration, we want to focus on raising it so that we're of the light and a more positive vibration- one that is involved in love, oneness, goodness, harmony, peace, and bliss. It's extremely important that if you want to live in a more positive state of mind and happiness, that you focus on the good aspects and qualities of light and live in a more good based reality rather than a fear based reality which is based on hate, no love and no light.

It is of utmost importance that you as a person begin to live in a higher state of awareness and begin to raise your vibration with the way you live, think, feel, eat and sleep. You can't focus on the negative fear-based actions which is hate, confusion, angst, fear, depression or anxiety. Living in awareness and light is about having a much higher state of consciousness and it's something that is imperative in order to attain a true state of positivity and love.

Living in a higher vibration is just living on a different and much higher vibrational plane of existence. It's functioning and existing in the plane of love and light and the higher vibrational frequencies, instead of the lower vibrational frequencies which is what usually happens to most people and a place many people end up resorting to and getting stuck in. You're generally functioning and raising your vibration to the light and a higher light and energetic frequency, and you are able to be of love and light moreso than those who are in a lower vibrational frequency.

Some specific ways to raise your vibration are to

1. Meditate and practice mindfulness and quietness. You can sit in a quiet place and contemplate to yourself for a certain period each day. There are specific kinds of

meditations that are around that can allow you to generate positive vibes and raise your energetic frequency.

2. Practice self-care: It is very important to focus on taking care of yourself each and every single day. Spend time outside with nature or read a book. This will help generate positive emotions and positive vibrations.

3. Think positive thoughts: keep your thoughts as positive and beneficial as possible, rather than thinking negative things, focus only on the positive. This will assist you with raising your vibration in a huge way and allow you to steer clear of the lower vibrational areas which are full of dark energies and lower ideas and concepts.

4. Explore spiritual arenas- there are many different means by which you can access Spiritual ideations and beliefs, and a few of them including taking up- spiritual classes And lessons, reading religious texts, take up yoga, meditate, along with many other Spiritual areas you can find in order to become an amazing high-vibrational person.

5. Eat high-vibrational food- eat healthy foods that have high vibrations such as Vegetables, fruits, and high fiber products, and other kinds of healthy meals which Will raise your vibration and cut down on junk foods and other types that will Lower your vibration.

6. Surround yourself with other high-vibrational people. It's important to surround Yourself with high vibrational people who actually spend time doing the exact Same things, and who take care of themselves and their bodies and those who focus On living their life in a positive and even a spiritual manner and who are happy People who can spread their love and happiness to you.

Once you spiritually awaken as well, you can gain a greater awareness and function in the higher arenas of frequency. People that function on a higher vibration are of a specific nature and once you're able to function on that vibrational level, you too can possess these qualities and traits. Some traits that these people do possess are empathy, compassion, forgiveness, healthy boundaries, good health, and an overall positive lifestyle and vibration. People with lower vibrational frequencies possess traits of being too depressed, anxious, self-critical, have a host of mental health and other issues, may have substance abuse issues and are functioning in a lower vibrational and very dark plane as opposed to one of the light.

Ways to gain a higher awareness:

There are various ways a person can gain a higher awareness or attain a more positive state of mind. A higher awareness is just being more mindful of that which is occurring in your life or around you. People with a higher awareness simply have a greater understanding of most concepts and have much better observation abilities once they have gained a higher awareness. You also possess a better understanding of the universe and world and many processes within it.

Some of these ways is through meditation, breathing exercises, basking yourself in sunlight, and just reading religious texts or verses. Other ways a person can gain a higher awareness is by focusing on nature in different aspects even while meditating. There are various ways to meditate, and this can help you gain a greater awareness and help you achieve a form of enlightenment. Breathing exercises are a really great way of being able to achieve a higher awareness or through meditation and there are different methods you can accomplish this. Another way to gain a higher awareness is to spiritually awaken in some form and there are many different ways of doing this.

Also, to gain a higher awareness you can become very observant of your surroundings and focus on every thought and action you take, and this can assist you with gaining a greater and higher awareness of aspects in your life and around you. You'll want to become incredibly aware of each and every action you take and make in your life, and this helps you become increasingly aware of all that is within you and all that is that surrounds you as well.

Gaining a higher awareness is also getting a higher consciousness, and ways of doing this including meditation, being healthy, being around other positive healthy spiritual people, repeat positive affirmations to yourself, pray to God and just pray in general, listen to spiritual and positive music or tones, play musician instruments, practice self-care, embrace nature and all that is beautiful in this world, let go of any fear based thinking that you hold-there is no purpose to living in a fear-based reality for it only hinders you and brings you down, so really steer away from that kind of thinking, focus on your third eye and even opening up and cleansing out your chakras, listen to yourself and get to know yourself better, learn a greater understanding of introspection, be mindful and present of each and every action and know exactly what actions you are undertaking. If you do these things, you're on your way to gaining a greater and much higher awareness and once you achieve this, you can do anything and hold the key to true happiness, love and positivity.

Chapter 5

CORE BELIEFS IN YOURSELF

How do you truly feel about yourself? Do you feel you're an accomplished person who has done all the things you can do in life? In order to truly attain happiness in our world and reality we basically have to understand the world and feelings that we possess about our own selves. We must understand how we feel about ourselves, others and how it relates to our true selves and the way we live our lives and how we function.

Do you believe in yourself as a human and all the amazing things you're able to accomplish? Or do you feel you're just not good enough to do simple tasks that seem difficult but really aren't too hard to do. If you picked the second response, you're like most others. Many people tend to feel this way for some reason, and they feel they're just not good enough to do or accomplish the things they're meant to accomplish in life or in general, or be able to do the things they're truly able to do. However, coming to a better understanding of what someone is able to accomplish is one of the few keys that a person can come to terms with to allow them to become greater people and achieve and accomplish more in their lives and become happier more fulfilled people.

The concept of happiness and truth can be achieved through our very core beliefs and values and the very way we actually feel about our own selves and the ways we function and exist in life. Setting core beliefs for yourself involves introspection and reflection on your values, experiences, and principles. You will need to consider your moral compass, personal growth, and the impact you'll want to make in the world.

How do you feel about yourself? Do you feel you're capable and able to do things that seem too difficult or daunting or do you tend to do well when it comes to your own core beliefs in yourself?

How we perceive ourselves and what we're capable of doing is an extremely important part of our lives and is one of the few most important ways we can elevate our levels of happiness and live happier, healthier lives.

1. Do you feel you're capable of doing difficult tasks

2. How do you perceive yourself overall or in general

3. Are you a positive or negative person?

4. How do you perceive your goals and accomplishments?

5. What is your self-worth like?

These are some of the questions you'll need to ask yourself when it comes to attempting to understand the beliefs and core feelings you have about yourself.

Your core beliefs in yourself are an integral part of your make up and a very important part of determining your current state of mind and what you're able to accomplish in life and your current perception of life.

Core beliefs shape our actions by serving as guiding principles and influencing our decision-making process. When our actions align with our core beliefs, we tend to feel a sense of authenticity, purpose, and fulfillment. Our core beliefs can motivate us to act in ways that are consistent with our values, and they can also help us navigate challenges and make choices that are in line with what we believe is right or important.

Common core beliefs can vary greatly among individuals, but some examples include beliefs in honesty, kindness, fairness, respect for others, personal responsibility, equality, empathy, and the pursuit of knowledge and personal growth. These are just a few examples, and everyone's core beliefs can be unique to their own experiences and values.

Core beliefs can change over time. As we grow, learn, and experience new things, our perspectives and values can evolve. Life events, new information, and personal growth can all contribute to shifts in our core beliefs. It's important to regularly reassess and reflect on our beliefs to ensure they align with who we are and who we want to become.

Getting to know yourself

Getting to know yourself is an extremely important part of trying to find who you are and engaging how you feel as a person and ultimately finding that true happiness within yourself. It's extremely important for you to know who you are and the things that encompass you as a human being. You are a wonderful blessing and a good person and somebody who deserves all the happiness in the world. Many times, people often second-guess themselves or doubt their own abilities, and they feel as if they are just not good enough to obtain any form of happiness or to even feel happy there are people that feel they don't even deserve happiness because they've reached certain points in Lowe's, which they ordinarily would not have gone to gotten to.

Do you often find yourself doubting your abilities and capabilities in general? Or do you just feel like you're not good enough to do specific or certain tasks? Take heed- you're definitely not the only one! There are millions like you who feel this same way. In fact, over 85 percent of Americans tend to doubt their own selves and beliefs! Do you feel you're just not good enough to accomplish the amazing things you're set out to do or do you feel you can find more out there? There are many others like you however this is exactly what you'll need to figure out and understand about yourself in order to gain a greater sense of happiness a deeper meaning of yourself and a greater understanding of your life and world.

Do you feel you're capable of doing difficult tasks?

Do you feel you're capable of doing difficult tasks? This is actually one question many people have about themselves, and one scenario that people tend to have a huge issue with. Most people just don't feel as if they're good enough to do daunting or difficult fields or tasks, and they feel as if they don't possess the talents or abilities to accomplish certain things in life or many things. There are many obstacles that people challenge themselves with, and the truth is that most people actually create these obstacles for themselves, rather than thinking in a positive and happy form and feeling as if they are able to accomplish these incredibly difficult or daunting tasks or things in life.

For instance, many people might want to get a higher degree, but they feel as if they're not good enough to do it. They simply feel as if they don't possess the culpability or capability to go to school, work hard, and do the things necessary in order to possess or obtain a specific kind of degree. There are people in life who seek to become great athletes or strive for this, but just feel as if they don't possess the capability or the idea or concept of being able to work hard enough to achieve these goals. This goal. The truth is each and every individual and each and every person out there is able to accomplish anything they put their mind to and they're actually able to do many of these Which they feel they don't believe they're able to do.

In order for you to achieve and attain true happiness, and elevate your levels of happiness you will have to change your core beliefs about yourself, and create a new and greater understanding of what you're capable enable to do. The way of doing these things is by actually taking on the tasks that you feel you're unable to do and accomplishing them and proving to yourself that you actually are able to do these things and not allowing fear-based emotions or fear-based concerns get to you.

How do you perceive yourself? Do you feel that you are a capable human being who is able to do all the things that you're able to do or do you feel as if you're just a failure or somebody who doesn't have it in you to do all these amazing great things that you may or to do or even simple things that you may, or may not seek to do?

What has created this perception of yourself have you failed at things in life? Have things not gone well for you? Have you attempted these tasks before or goals and for some reason they just didn't work out for you and you didn't seem to accomplish them, or finish what you had to do. It's extremely important that we don't second-guess or ourselves or downplay what we're actually capable of it's extremely important that we learn to believe in our own gifts and talents, and in our own capabilities this is the key and foundation for us to succeed in life, and for us to elevate our levels of happiness and goodness and also for us to further ourselves and progress in our own wonderful lives.

Our lives are extremely important and life is very short so it's important for us much as we can, and do so on this planet with a short time or the time that we are given, and it's important for us to have the correct perception of our own abilities and talents in order for us to succeed in life and move forward for if we don't, then we basically are going to continue second-guessing ourselves and never accomplish the wonderful things that were able to do. Having the correct perception of yourself. and the more positive outlook of your own abilities and talents, and what you're actually able to accomplish and what you're capable of is extremely important. It's very important that we don't second-guess ourselves and feel as if we're just not good enough to certain things in life when we actually have the capability of doing almost anything we want to do.

So how do you perceive yourself overall or in general? Do you feel that you're good enough to do just about anything? Do you feel that you're able to do many things in life? does life go by for you pretty easily? or are things extremely difficult for you? Well, this is a question, and these are many questions that many people do have about themselves. People have a general concern somewhere within themselves, and the truth is that most people tend to doubt what their capabilities are, and their perception of themselves is extremely flawed. The most important thing and concept of understanding is that your perception of yourself needs to be completely accurate, and it shouldn't be flawed or confused the way it usually is for most people.

We as humans tend to be very confused about what our own capabilities, and what our own talents and gifts are. We live in states of confusion, and lack of knowing what reality truly is and that's because we're living in a bubble of that which we truly do not know. We're unable to know what our what we're actually capable and truly able to do. Do you perceive, so how do you perceive yourself? This is one of the most important questions that you'll ask yourself, and you will have to come to a greater understanding of the truth of who you truly are and how amazing and great your abilities really are!

Are you a positive or negative person?

So, are you a positive or negative person? Are you a person that wakes up and that lives and goes throughout your day and a very positive and happy manner? Do you go throughout your day thinking happy positive thoughts and thoughts that actually enhancer day and make it better than it normally would be or are you a person that actually thinks in negative tones, and. Escalates on these negative tones, and has an as affected by the negative ways that occur in your life?

Are you given the ability to be a positive person, or do you possess the unfortunate concept of being more of a negative person? Whether you're a positive or negative person it doesn't change the fact that your capabilities in life are going to be what you're able to do however, the means of your being able to accomplish an obtain these goals is going to change based on your outlook and the kind of person you are.

Most of the time, if you're a positive person, you're hopefully going to think in a very positive, happy way and that positivity tends to assist you with your daily tasks in life and it allows you to be a more successful person constantly in a state of self-doubt, fear, confusion, angst and the things that are going to affect you in a negative way rather than be of a positive influence and that's going to affect your life and hinder your goals in some form. It is extremely important that you focus more on being a positive person, and snowballing the positive effects that you can have on your own life rather than being a negative person, and focusing on self-doubt, fear, and all those negative qualities that are going to bring you down and pretty much upset or affect your life in a and a hugely negative or downward manner.

Do you think in tones of "I can't do this" or "I don't feel I'm good enough for this?" Well then you tend to be more of a negative person and it's very important that you don't focus on these negative feelings and ideations, and that you focus on being a positive happy person, because that positivity is actually going to allow you to be happier to allow you to discover your inner great and hidden talents, and allow you to live a more and blissful life, rather than being in states of doubt and fear and confusion.

So how do you perceive your goals and accomplishments in life do you actually have goals and accomplishments in life or do you feel as if you've accomplished all the things you want to accomplish and your six content in life and you don't really want to do much more? Have you just not accomplished anything in life basically and want to keep it that way? This is a confusing topic to talk about because not everybody is going to have accomplishments and goals they want to pursue in life. However, many people actually do have many goals that they do would like that they would like to pursue.

Are you a person who feels as if there are many things that you would like to do in life would you like to accomplish many things and for some reason you're just unable to do these things or do you feel as if you are extremely successful as you are or content with the way you are? it's important to understand what our goals and accomplishments are in order for us to further understand who we are. It's important to understand who we are as people and why we're on this planet and what we are there to do as far as helping ourselves and helping others as well. Many of us aren't on this planet simply to work and eat and live mundane random lives. We actually have other goals that we would like to accomplish and it's extremely important as a person that you understand what your limp capabilities are when what your limitations are and what your goals in life are in order to further understand who you are as a person.

For most of us, the sky is the limit and it's something that we don't fully understand as humans we truly feel as if we are limited in the things that were able to do we feel as if there's so much that we want to do but so much that we're just unable to do for some reason And we actually limit ourselves because the truth is that our capabilities are unlimited and we're able to do almost anything that we set our mind to and there are hundreds and thousands of feats and tasks that we as humans are actually Able to accomplish. We need to understand what our goals are in life and in order to do this you will just need to sit down and write your goals and what you would like to do in life and from there on you'll need to understand and perceive what you need to do in order to achieve those goals in order to move forward and build upon that and this will allow you to become a happier and healthier person and allow you to understand yourself on a greater level than what you're normally used to.

What is your self-worth like?

One extremely important key characteristic to better understanding yourself, and in order to grow your happiness, and know more about who you are to be a positive person is to understand yourself self-worth. What is your self-worth like? Do you love yourself or do you look down on yourself? Do you love yourself but feel as if you're just limited and many things that you can do in life? Do you have high self-esteem, or do you have low self-esteem? These are just some of the questions you can ask yourself, and a few things that you can do to write down in order to discover how you truly feel about yourself and how you can person and how you perceive self-worth. it is extremely important to have a self-esteem and sense of self-worth because you are actually an amazing great creation of God and you deserve to understand and know that you matter your life matters, and that your self-worth is something that is extremely high in extreme importance and not something that is very low. You must discover that upon yourself you must look at yourself and judge and analyze what kind of self-worth you do have, and how you perceive your own self and what self-esteem is like.

One of the most important concepts that we must possess in our own life is the understanding of our own worth, and our own importance so for this exercise, you will need to just write down all the good qualities about yourself and you'll need to write down all the negative qualities about yourself and gauge and see how you perceive your own self-worth because this is extremely important for you to understand and get a greater understanding of yourself. This will allow you to know yourself better, and to steer yourself in the direction of goodness, positivity, and a happier and better outlook on life.

And allow you to further accomplish your goals, and all the things that you've always wanted to accomplish in life. This is just one of the few things that will allow you to do that just that. it's extremely important that you perceive your own self-worth for what it is and that you build on your self-worth with positivity and goodness, and you can do that through positive affirmations, and reminding yourself of many good things that you do possess and that do you can accomplish on this planet.

Chapter 6

Ways To Harness Positive Energy

It's important to focus on anything positive in one's life and to reflect upon that, rather than worrying about the negative things occurring in someone's general reality.

Positivity and optimistic thinking is in fact a major snowball effect that just builds on itself once it begins. You have to generate positive thinking and energy and this positive state of mind in everything that you do, in everything that you exist in or in anything you partake of or are a part of. You have to emphasize and focus on the positive aspects of any event you're going to partake in or be a part of.

If you're going to a party don't focus on the fear based aspects such as "what will happen once I get there," will it be fun, will there be anyone to talk to, will there be any conflicts or disagreements? Think of the party or event as a fun positive social experience you're about to have with friends and others who are good positive kind people. Focus on being friendly and generating positive vibes.

Positivity is extremely contagious, and you must harness and cultivate a positive state of mind in order to live your life with a positive enlightened state of mind and in order to cultivate good energy in everything that you do and within every aspect of your life. Stop thinking based on fears, hesitancies, worries or any other fear based programmed ideations or concepts. If you can't get the fear-based concepts out of your mind, keep them in the. Background and try to eliminate them as much as possible. Anything fear based usually tends to create that very scenario that you fear may occur or that which you don't want to happen.

Humanity was not designed to be created to fear things that occur in life. Society has turned into a fear based platform only because of the nature of concepts that occur on a daily basis. Tests, exams, job interviews, schedules, work, hierarchies create a general fear based atmosphere and people tend to abide by these rules and concepts.

Rather than focusing on the fear involved in all of these concepts, it's important to focus on the power of positivity and love within every task you undertake or any ordeal that you are challenged with.

Cultivating positive energy is the most important aspect of harnessing positive energy and being a happy person. There are various ways of harnessing positive energy and snowballing its effects. In order to be a happy person, you will need to learn and practice how to do this. You will need to build upon focusing on being a positive and happy good person. In order to do this, you'll need to take an experience, event or a moment you're in and just be positive and in the moment, and then focus on all the positive qualities of that particular event or moment and build upon them in a major way. Continue focusing on the positive aspect of that event and focus on building positive energy as well. This is just one of the few ways you can actually build on creating good energy and positivity for a specific cause or purpose.

It's incredibly important to cultivate and harness and build on a positive experience that you've had. You can do this energetically, and in many other ways.

1. Build a shield of positive energy by snowballing positive energies around you
2. Focus on the good aspects in your life or events/experiences
3. Enhance any positive energy or experiences that you currently do have
4. Appreciate nature and all there is to experience
5. Engage in deep breathing exercises
6. Meditate and focus on spirituality
7. Hang around like-minded and very positive people
8. Eat healthy and high vibrational foods to help build positive energies

It's very important to build upon any aspect of positivity and good energy that you can. It may seem difficult at first, but rest assured it does get much easier. Being a positive and happy person is something that can be done easily on a whim even if you haven't had much practice. However, extreme practice can turn you into an expert when it comes to being an incredibly positive person and someone who can turn something negative into something positive right away!

So, cultivating positive energy is the concept of actually enhancing positive energy that's in an area of surface or space, and just making it more and more enhanced than it normally would be.

Positive energy is a wonderful great effect of a beautiful energy, snowball effect that gets greater and greater with each element.

There are other ways to harness positive energy. Some methods include practicing gratitude, surrounding yourself with positive people and environments, engaging in activities that bring you joy, taking care of your physical and mental well-being, and cultivating a positive mindset through affirmations and positive self-talk.

Some examples of gratitude practices include keeping a gratitude journal and writing down things you are grateful for each day, expressing gratitude to others through thank-you notes or verbal appreciation, taking a moment each day to mentally acknowledge and appreciate the things you are grateful for, and practicing mindfulness by focusing on the present moment and finding gratitude in the small things around you.

Focus on the Minor Positives

Being a positive person and having a positive state of mind isn't always an easy task. It's extremely important that you start off with focusing on the positives and work your way into having a completely positive state of mind and thinking positively and good, amazing thoughts with each and everything you do and with everything that happens in your wonderful, amazing life. Your life is a wonderful, amazing gift given to you by your Creator and given to you by your parents and something that you should be thrilled to experience and love each and every second of your life. Life isn't a mundane sad experience, or a boring pointless confusing experience like many people tend to believe it is. Everything you do in your life is a new discovery, a new brilliant fun experience for you and yourself and for those in your life who you love and who are blessed to be around you! Each and every second of your life can be an amazing experience for you to enjoy and bask in it's every second of glory and amazement.

You might say, well how is that possible if I "go to the same job each and every day" "talk to the same people", "eat in the same place." Well, that is because each and every day is incredibly different of course and each and every experience is different even though it seems the same. You can still enjoy all of these great experiences whether they seem to be the same or not. That is what being a positive happy person entails- it literally entails enjoying every experience in your life differently even if it seems the same, or whether it's different or not. One of the few ways you can begin to do this Is to focus on the minor positives. It's extremely important to focus on the minor positives in your life. It's also important to just make each and every experience in your life incredibly amazing and fun, which may not always seem possible, but it is.

Of course, that's how most people tend to live life, but not everyone has the same set of standards or the same state of mind. For example, Jennifer a female who works at her job, might enjoy going to work and going to her job, interacting with her co-workers, and just being a good employee and might enjoy doing the same thing each and every single day. However, she may not be focusing on the positives. Part of focusing on the positives in your life, is having a higher awareness or a higher state of mind and vibration and that will be talked about in another chapter.

Focus on the good aspects in your life

Focus on the really good things happening in your life. It's a good idea to focus on the great qualities and events happening in your life and build upon them. If there is a good event or something taking place, then you'll need to elevate that experience and build upon and focus on all the positive qualities of that event or aspect in your life. If you have a good job, a great family, a good support group and network of friends, or any of those then feel grateful and blessed for having those things and be thrilled and then look to those good things happening in your life and focus on the positives regarding those. Think of every good thing in your life and write those things out and then focus on each of those things in your life and why you're so grateful for them. This is a very helpful way of being and staying positive and getting into a positive state of mind.

Cultivating a positive state of mind involves shifting your thoughts and perspectives into more positive ones that include the concept of reframing and being around positive influences and challenging negative beliefs. It does take time and effort to do this.

The power of positivity refers to the impact that a positive mindset and attitude can have on our well-being and on our quality of life. It can increase motivation, improve our mental states, and attract more positive experiences in our life. The power of positivity is a powerful belief in the power that positivity is the key to healing and helping many ailments that afflict our society and that are there to cause issues for us. Positivity can help improve your mental and physical health and well-being, cope with stress and achieve your goals. It is a wonderful habit that can be learned and practiced- by developing self-compassion skills or through achievements and goals in life.

Harnessing a positive mindset and practicing positivity can bring on numerous benefits such as reduced stress levels, improved mental and emotional well-being, increased resilience in the face of challenges, greater relationships and social connections, better physical health, increased motivation and a greater sense of overall happiness and life satisfaction. Having a wonderful positive state of mind can have tremendous positive health benefits as well and can heal many different ailments and health issues such as reducing stress,, improving immune function, better cardiovascular health, and support of overall mental and physical health, greater resistance to the common cold, increased physical well-being, longer life span, lower rates of depression, reduced risk of cardiovascular disease.

Chapter 7

THE KEY TO HAPPINESS

So, what is happiness and what is the key to happiness and positivity? That's a question that many people out there ask and wonder for themselves. People can't fully understand what the concept of happiness really is and that's because most people have never attained or achieved true happiness and they don't know what the feeling really is and what the concept means. Happiness isn't just a feeling or a lifestyle. There is so much more to what being a happy person is, and what being a happy positive person is, and what the concept of happiness is. We live in a world, full of selfishness, greed, confusion, angst, anxiety, depression, trauma, and so many negative qualities that many people have forgotten what the concept of what happiness truly is, and how to attain that nirvana of happiness, and how to be happy once again.

Happiness is the key to living a beautiful, wonderful, gracious life, full of joy and bliss, and one of the few ways of being happy is by being an extremely positive wonderful, generous, gracious human being, and not everybody possesses the quality of being positive or happy. Many people don't possess these qualities and they don't really know where to begin when it comes to gauging their own happiness, and most people lack a common concept, known as introspection, and they lack the concept of knowing who they are deep within way of gaining and elevating.

Your happiness is by knowing who you are within yourself, and many people just lack this knowledge or concept in general. Happiness is the joy and beauty that we live on a day-to-day basis and it's the graciousness that we possess in our everyday lives. It's the positivity that we surround ourselves within, that we even obtain that we attain to desiring, and that which we desire most; however, it's not something that everybody actually possesses and it's something that we all need to understand on a greater level and elevate regardless of what level of state we're in in life.

I was personally never that depressed of a person, but I did experience some depression in my teenage years, and after many years of a spiritual awakening, I found myself in a standstill of possessing an abundance of bliss, energy, and happiness, and glory and graciousness. We live in a world where many people do possess the concept of depression, gloominess, darkness and really it's not beneficial to live this way. It's not beneficial to be of a dark person and have to live this kind of lifestyle when you actually can possess the concept of happiness. It's also extremely important to be a positive and happy person rather than being something that might be negative, dark or gloomy, whether you're accustomed to it or not.

The key to happiness is basking in a constant and beautiful, amazing state of positivity, glory, love, and light, for all that is out there for the Creator God, and for that which has been created and elevating in building on this positivity. Also, being a beautiful, wonderful, good human being. These are some of the few keys to being a happy, wonderful and enlightened human being.

I was once a depressed person however, this only occurred in my teenage years, though I do remember feeling what it was like to possess the concept of depression and that was definitely not a fun time to experience, and those were not wonderful feelings to have.

However, as I grew to be an adult, I learned through many experiences, life lessons, and even through a spiritual awakening what the concept of true happiness is, and the idea of being a truly happy person in living in the moment and being in an elevated state of happiness. Harnessing that which is positive is an extremely important part of being a happy person and also cultivating a positive state of mind and reminding yourself of your blessings, and all the gracious amazing things that you do possess all your possessions your gifts, the love that you have your friends, family and wonderful support system. These are just a few things that allow you to reap the rewards of being a happy fruitful, amazing human being.

The key and truth to happiness is a greater understanding of yourself a higher awareness, full introspection, great spiritual abilities or spirituality cultivating beauty, love, light and positivity. Elevating in building on that and focusing on that which is positive and your blessings and your love and light are just a few key ways you can be a happier healthier and more beautiful you, and one of the few ways you can bask in the glory of happiness, love and light.

Another way to happiness is through the gift of love, and is one of the few concepts that we must understand and possess in order to attain a greater understanding and meaning of the concept of happiness. Once we fully possess the beauty of love within ourselves, we will then flow into being, happier, more positive people who can accomplish, and do anything that we want and succeed in life, and just live each and every moment in our daily lives through the lens of happiness and love. Our blessings are elevated daily and within each moment and it is extremely important that we focus on this love and harmony through the gift of peace and joy, and this is one of the few ways you can actually elevate your positivity and joy. Your personal and true happiness is through the gift and lens of love.

One of the few keys to happiness is by spreading love and light now what is love and light you might ask? Love and light are actually eternal love and bliss and it's something that not everybody feels but it's something that everybody has access to, and we are all true love and light deep within ourselves. We can access this love and light whenever we need to, and this is actually one of the few ways that we can be happiness and spread positivity within ourselves, and to others as well.

Now, we are the keys to our own happiness. The key to happiness is actually our own selves, and that's another way we can actually access our own souls, and the loving light that is within us, and that is through the loving light within our souls. This is also another integral way that we can build on the positivity through the beauty of our souls, because the soul is the key to our eternal selves.

We are the beauty and light that we seek. We actually possess this amazing beauty and light within ourselves, and we are the key to our own happiness. We are beauty, love, light, wonder and real amazement, and we are the ones that possess the keys to our own happiness, and to unlimited happiness and elevated states of happiness, where we can build on what we possess when it comes to the concept of happiness.

Getting to know you:

It is very important that you get to know you. Getting to know yourself is an extremely important part of raising your awareness, levels of introspection, vibration and your overall happiness. You are the MOST important element in your universe and getting to know yourself is one element of extreme self-care and something that is very important for you to do, in order to achieve many of the gracious goals that you'll want to achieve or accomplish in your daily life.

Getting to know yourself is a wonderful way of practicing extreme self-care and understanding exactly who you are and all the wonderful qualities that you possess and also understanding what your limitations are, how you function, and how you think and how you perceive your life and day-to-day life in general. It is extremely important for a person to know who they are how they think and what their life is like and how they manage and perceive every aspect of life in general.

Are you a happy person in general or are you more negative or down?

Are you a person who looks to the future for brighter things or do you make things happen in your own life? Well, many people actually expect good or great things to happen in their life. They actually think that maybe good things are going to happen in their life or positive things will happen, and then they might be disappointed when negative things actually do happen, so you definitely don't want to have the state of mind of hoping that positive things come your way, and that good things will happen in your life. You want to have the state of mind of actually making those things happen, and allowing your own self to be this powerhouse of positivity that allows things to occur in your life. You want to be the vessel to allow things to happen in your life, and to make things happen rather than wait for positive things to come into your world and into your life. Positive things will come your way in life, once you begin to make it happen for yourself and then the sky is the limit for you once the ball gets rolling and you make those great things come to fruition.

It's extremely important that you focus on these things that you focus on making positive and things happen good things happen in your life, rather than waiting for them to happen on their own. Most of the time, if you wait for good things to happen to you they usually won't happen. It's up to you to take the necessary steps to planning your life goals and implementing them and making them happen to you. This is one of the few keys to success and happiness in this world.

One really good exercise for you to do is to write down a list of positive and negative things in your life list all the positives on one line, and all the negatives on another line and then with the positives you need to list more positives and positive happy things about all the positive wonderful things in your life. This will allow you to elevate and understand and increase in number, all the happy great things that are currently in your life, and happening in your life. It is extremely important to add to this and to allow yourself to add more goals and more ideas and elements into your positive side and to focus on those making those things happen as well.

Do you have goals in life that you haven't accomplished yet? Are there things in your life that you want to do that you haven't done? Maybe you feel as if you're not good enough to do those things or you don't believe in yourself well now is the time to start believing in yourself! You are the only one that can allow all these positive events and experiences to take place and happen. There is nobody else that will allow these things to happen except for yourself. You are the only one who can make all these positive goals, life, events, and life goals come to fruition. You are the only person that can allow these things to happen.

Finding a sense of purpose in life

Another key to happiness can be finding a sense of purpose in your life. Most people tend to live mundane and bleak lives by their own standards and definition and it's important to figure out what your sense of purpose in this life and world are. This is a personal journey and it can involve exploring your passions, values, strengths, and aligning them with meaningful goals. It's important to reflect on what brings you joy, and how you can contribute to your society and the world around you.

Doing charity work can also help a person gain a greater sense of purpose in life and allow one to boost or increase their levels of positivity and happiness. Helping others is a wonderful, gracious, and beneficial task that a person can do on this planet, and it can definitely help a person gain a greater sense of purpose in life and allow them to become more positive and happier people by helping others and making others happy in the process and being of benefit to others.

A sense of purpose can change over time and maybe in the past a person had a different feeling or belief in their purpose in life, yet as they grew and learned and had new experiences things changed for them. It's important to understand and explore what your current sense of purpose is and why you feel you're on this planet and what you feel you're here to accomplish in life.

Having goals in life is important as well and aligning goals with a sense of purpose means that you set objectives that are meaningful for your values and passions. It's important to make sure that your goals in life are in alignment with your sense of purpose and important to know that your sense of purpose will evolve as you get older and have more and more experiences in life.

In order to rediscover your sense of purpose, you will need to contemplate on self-reflection, exploration and experimenting with various activities and events in your wonderful life. What tends to bring you joy and fulfillment and what values do you hold that are important to you exclusively? You'll want to engage in brand new and fun experiences, and seek out different ideals in life, and also be very open-minded into trying out new things if you want to rediscover your purpose in life.

Engaging in activities that bring joy and fulfillment can easily increase one's happiness and are some of the major keys to happiness as well. This can include hobbies, spending time with loved ones, practicing mindfulness or meditation, exercising, pursuing personal goals, helping others through acts of kindness, and seeking out experiences that bring you a sense of meaning and purpose.

Experiment with different activities to find what resonates with you the most.

Cultivating positive relationships can assist with one's positive energy levels and improving someone's quality of life. It's a good thing if you're able to see the glass as half-full and if you're a positive person who knows how to effectively hold positive and beneficial relationships, rather than ones full of negativity, despair, anger, or hostility. Ways to cultivate positive relationships include effective communication skills, active listening, empathy, and mutual respect. Invest time and effort in building and maintaining connections, show genuine interest in others, be supportive, and prioritize quality time together. It's important to have a good listening ear and be an empathetic and kind caring person rather than a selfish one who doesn't care for the other person's needs, concerns or wants. Open and honest communication is key, and it's important to resolve conflicts in a healthy and positive manner.

Chapter 8

HEALING PAST TRAUMAS AND FEARS

Healing from past trauma is a complex and individual process. It often involves seeking support from professionals, such as therapists or counselors, who can provide guidance and therapeutic techniques. Self-care practices, such as mindfulness, exercise, and engaging in activities that bring you joy, can also be helpful. It's important to be patient with yourself and allow the healing process to unfold at its own pace.

There are several therapy approaches commonly used for healing trauma, including Cognitive Behavioral Therapy (CBT), Eye Movement Desensitization and Reprocessing (EMDR), Trauma-Focused Cognitive Behavioral Therapy (TF-CBT), and Dialectical Behavior Therapy (DBT). These approaches can really help individuals process and cope with traumatic experiences, manage symptoms, and promote healing and resilience. The choice of therapy approach may depend on the specific needs and preferences of the individual.

Cognitive Behavioral Therapy (CBT) can help with trauma by addressing negative thought patterns and behaviors that may be contributing to distress. It focuses on identifying and challenging distorted or disordered thinking patterns, developing coping skills to manage distressing emotions, and exposes individuals to trauma-related triggers in a very safe controlled manner. CBT really aims to reduce trauma symptoms and promote adaptive coping strategies. CBT involves setting goals, learning new skills, and practicing new techniques and ways to reframe irrational or negative thoughts and beliefs. Therapists and clients work together to develop effective and beneficial strategies for managing symptoms and improving the overall well-being of the client.

Healing past trauma involves addressing and resolving the emotional, psychological, and physical impacts of traumatic experiences. It often involves processing and integrating the memories and emotions associated with the trauma, developing coping strategies, and fostering resilience. Healing can lead to a reduction in symptoms, improved overall well-being, and a sense of empowerment and growth.

Healing past fears can involve gradually confronting and processing the underlying causes of these fears. There are techniques used to do this such as gradual exposure therapy, cognitive restructuring, and relaxation techniques that can be helpful and aim at doing an effective job of this. It's also important to get support from a psychotherapist or counselor.

Letting go of past fears can be a gradual process. There are steps that come with this that include understanding the fears, challenging negative thoughts and beliefs associated with them and gradually exposing yourself to situations that trigger the fear in a very safe and controlled way. Seeking help from a therapist or guidance from a counselor can help too. Also being self-compassionate and patient can assist with the process of getting go of past fears.

There are self-help techniques that can aid in healing past fears. These include deep breathing exercises, journaling, mindfulness, and meditation practices, getting support from friends or family members and being a part of activities that focus on relaxation and self-care. Also seeking professional help from a therapist would be one of the best routes for getting help with deep-rooted fears.

Healing past traumas and fears is not always an easy feat to do. There are many awful and difficult circumstances that a person might have to undergo, and there are also various ways a person can heal from these situations. Traumas can manifest in many different forms and things are extremely difficult and painful for a person to have to endure and deal with. Traumas are basically painful past situations, experiences, or circumstances that a person has had to undergo that have created a very painful memory or recollection of and something that a person usually would need therapy for or other forms of healing in order to let go of the situation or not let them affect their current life.

Healing can be very difficult to do when it comes to specific kinds of traumas and it's not always easy to let go of the negativity or fear that the traumatic event has caused a person. Healing is a complex modality and means of assisting with handling traumas and other experiences that someone has had to deal with. The concept of healing is not always a simple task to undergo. Traumas are generally rooted in extreme fear, negativity, hatred, and other negative means of thinking and are generally deep-rooted in nature for a person.

In order to heal and help with past traumas a person needs to first understand the nature and root cause of the trauma and how it originated. A trauma basically happens if a person goes through a painful or difficult or traumatic type of experience or situation. Let's say Jennifer, a 28-year-old was sexually abused as a child and experienced a lot of childhood trauma and experiences and negativity as a result of the abuse she faced. As a result of the abuse, she dealt with, she is left to deal with a lot of trauma as the aftermath of the abuse she had to endure. The traumatic roots of her experiences have left her with extreme post-traumatic stress disorder, suicidal tendencies, and flashbacks of the experiences she had to undergo.

Healing these kinds of situations is definitely not an easy feat to have to deal with. There are many various methods and means of ways to heal traumatic experiences and remove them completely from a person's psyche and not let it affect them the way it has been. PTSD is a huge problem in the aftermath of a traumatic situation or event and many people experience PTSD in all kinds of various forms. PTSD is post-traumatic stress disorder and symptoms can actually start from one month to much later after the event occurs. This disorder can interfere with a person's ability to work, or even function in daily life. These symptoms can even get worse over time and need ways to be managed or cared for otherwise things can get really bad for the person dealing with these issues.

Treatments for PTSD include various forms of medication and psychotherapy treatment or a combination of both and they are usually the best forms or ways of dealing with PTSD or any form of major trauma. There are also alternative ways of dealing with trauma and fear-based issues that have arisen in a person's life, mind, and psyche.

Past traumas can have a huge impact on a person's life. They can greatly affect a person's day-to-day life and need to be taken care of when dealing with a person whose life is being affected by this. Focusing on being a positive person and focusing on changing your mindset from negativity to positivity can have a great impact when it comes to healing traumas or a fear-based state of mind.

Having an incredibly positive state of mind can assist with healing a fear-based state of mind. What exactly is a fear-based state of mind? This is when a person reacts and lives their life based on fear or other negative ideations rather than positive or wholesome good ones. Healing trauma and fear-based thinking needs to be done from the root of the issue and also from the cause that triggered these feelings in the first place. That is only when healing can take place.

If Jennifer had a traumatic sexual experience that took place as a child, then regression therapy would be one of the best modalities for healing this type of trauma. However, there are other ways a person can be healed as well. Going to the root of the trauma and talking about the very core scenario and dealing with the issues and processes that took place at the time is one of the better effective techniques to use to help heal any form of trauma or negative fear-based thinking.

However, there are other ways of incorporating healing using a positive state of mind, positive affirmations and the theory and technique of replacing negative thoughts and states of mind with positive and beneficial ones.

Healing from past trauma can be a complex process. There are many different techniques that can be used to help with trauma experiences. Here are just some general suggestions which allow a person to heal from trauma-based experiences.

1. Seek professional help: Consider working with a therapist or counselor experienced in trauma therapy to guide you through the healing process.
2. Practice self-care: Engage in activities that promote your physical, emotional, and mental well-being, such as exercise, relaxation techniques, and hobbies.
3. Build a support system: Surround yourself with understanding and supportive individuals who can provide empathy and encouragement. It's important to have a healthy support system of friends, family and others who can encourage and help you out.

4. Express emotions: Find healthy ways to express and process your emotions, such as through journaling, art, or talking with a trusted friend.
5. Educate yourself: Learn about trauma and its effects to gain a better understanding of your experiences and coping strategies.
6. Practice self-compassion: Be kind and patient with yourself as you navigate the healing journey, acknowledging that it takes time and effort.
7. Consider support groups: Joining a support group with others who have experienced similar trauma can provide a sense of validation and shared understanding.
8. Explore therapeutic techniques: Techniques like cognitive-behavioral therapy (CBT), eye movement desensitization and reprocessing (EMDR), or somatic experiencing may be beneficial in processing and healing trauma.
9. Engage in grounding exercises: Practice grounding techniques, such as deep breathing or mindfulness, to help manage distressing symptoms and stay present in the moment.
10. Set boundaries: Establish and enforce healthy boundaries to protect yourself from triggers or situations that may retraumatize you.

Remember, healing from trauma is a personal journey, and it's important to find approaches that work best for you.

There are many extremely effective ways that a person can go about healing trauma. Here are just a few good examples of these.

1. Cognitive-Behavioral Therapy (CBT): This therapy helps identify and challenge negative thoughts and beliefs related to the trauma, replacing them with healthier and more adaptive ones.
2. Eye Movement Desensitization and Reprocessing (EMDR): EMDR involves guided eye movements or other forms of bilateral stimulation to process traumatic memories and reduce their emotional impact.
3. Somatic Experiencing: This approach focuses on the physical sensations and bodily experiences associated with trauma, helping to release stored tension and promote healing.
4. Mindfulness and Meditation: These practices can help cultivate present-moment awareness, reduce anxiety, and promote emotional regulation.
5. Expressive Therapies: Engaging in creative outlets like art therapy, music therapy, or dance/movement therapy can provide a non-verbal means of processing and expressing trauma.

6. Trauma-Informed Yoga: Yoga practices specifically designed for trauma survivors can help regulate the nervous system, release tension, and promote a sense of safety and grounding.
7. Narrative Therapy: This approach involves exploring and reshaping the narrative of the traumatic experience, empowering individuals to reframe their story and find meaning and growth.

It's important to note that these techniques should be practiced under the guidance of a trained professional, as trauma healing can be complex and sensitive. Working with a therapist experienced in trauma treatment can provide personalized guidance and support throughout the healing process.

There are also many alternative or complementary approaches that are reality available that can assist individuals in healing trauma. These approaches may be used alongside or in addition to traditional therapies. Some examples include:

1. Acupuncture: This ancient Chinese practice involves the insertion of thin needles into specific points on the body to promote balance and healing.
2. Equine-Assisted Therapy: Interacting with horses under the guidance of a therapist can help individuals build trust, develop emotional regulation skills, and process trauma.

3. Herbal Supplements: Some individuals find certain herbal supplements, such as chamomile or lavender, helpful in managing anxiety or promoting relaxation.
4. Body-based Therapies: Practices like massage therapy, craniosacral therapy, or somatic experiencing can help release tension and promote healing through touch and body awareness.
5. Energy Healing: Modalities like Reiki or Healing Touch focus on balancing the body's energy and promoting relaxation and well-being.
6. Nature Therapy: Spending time in nature, engaging in activities like hiking or gardening, can provide a sense of calm, connection, and grounding.

It's important to remember that while these approaches may be beneficial for some individuals, they may not work for everyone. It's essential to consult with qualified practitioners and discuss any alternative or complementary approaches with your healthcare provider or therapist to ensure they align with your specific needs and circumstances.

How to Beat Depression:

Depression is a very severe and serious clinical mental illness and mental issue that's prevalent in over 280 million humans today. Depression can manifest in a variety of ways including lack of self-care, mental state of low mood and aversion to activity. Depression can affect a person's thoughts, behavior, feelings, sense of well-being. Depressed people often experience loss of motivation or interest in, or reduced pleasure or joy from, experiences that would normally bring them pleasure or joy. Depression is a serious illness and it's something that needs to be treated regularly with various medications and by a trained physician.

Depression is a mental health disorder characterized by persistent feelings of sadness, loss of interest or pleasure in activities, changes in appetite or sleep patterns, low energy, difficulty concentrating, and thoughts of worthlessness or guilt. It can affect a person's emotions, thoughts, and overall functioning, often requiring professional help for diagnosis and treatment.

Depression can have multiple causes, including a combination of genetic, biological, environmental, and psychological factors. Some common causes include a family history of depression, certain chemical imbalances in the brain, major life changes or stressful events, chronic medical conditions, certain medications, and a history of trauma or abuse. It's important to note that everyone's experience with depression is unique and the causes can vary from person to person.

It's important to understand the basis of depression and that people who are depressed have undergone varying kinds of issues, traumas and have a chemical imbalance within their system as well.

Depression can manifest as a serious chemical imbalance, and it can affect the nervous system in a serious way. People can have false beliefs about themselves, their own lives, and tend to withdraw in different ways once they have this particular illness. There are different ways to beat and fight depression and that involves having an extremely positive state of mind along with therapy and medication. Depressed people can have suicidal ideations and tendencies and are prone to getting in trouble and can have a whole host of problems that affect their everyday lives. Many people are non-functional and are unable to function in everyday society.

In order to assist people with depression, there are methods and ways of dealing with the situation at hand which include psychiatric medications and varying forms of therapy. Though these are all necessary forms and means of healing depression there are other ways that depression can be healed along with these modalities. One way that depression can be healed includes methods of natural healing which incorporate a positive state of mind and a positive way of thinking.

Depression is an illness that has affected over 280 million Americans today. It's a terrifying illness and it can affect a person in a variety a large number of different ways. Depression is something that can have a huge negative impact on a person however, there are a large number of ways that a person can actually handle their depression, or even beat or deal with depression.

A study of depressed people show that the majority of depressed people are really just searching for ways to ease or cure their illness, and that many of them are unable to handle this particular illness out of many other illnesses, or mental illnesses.

A wonderful way to heal or deal with clinical depression is actually the employment of extreme positive energy and this is something that you can use in various quantities and amounts in order to attempt to sort negative feelings, and the chemical imbalance that is going on with the seriousness of depression.

In order to treat depression, you have to go to the root cause you have to go to the root root of the problem and situation, and that stems from the exact events of what actually happened in the past. You will have to focus on extreme positive notions, along with healing, the root of the problem and employing a way to heal using extreme positivity, love and light.

The natural and positive ways of healing depression

Meditation is in fact an amazing way of dealing with beating and healing various forms of depression. There are numerous benefits to meditation, but most people just don't know that meditation actually has the greatest natural benefits for those suffering from depression. Studies have shown that depressed people actually have a very weak pre-frontal cortex area of the brain. The pre-frontal cortex portion of the brain is the emotional control center, and those diagnosed with depression actually have a weak cortex. A study by Harvard neuroscientist Dr. Sara Lazar showed that the brains of meditators had remarkably more "prefrontal cortex gray matter thickness", which was linked directly to meditation practice.

Studies have shown that the chemical imbalance issue of depression affects your brainwave patterns, and that meditation can have the healthiest most positive effects on your brainwaves. The Biofeedback Institute did a study on 14 clinically depressed alcoholics as they were given experimental alpha and theta brainwave therapy over the course of multiple sessions.

To measure their results, each participant took a "Beck Depression Inventory Score" before and after the experiment. The results they found were astounding.

The participants, in fact, reduced their depression score by 80% (21-pre, 4-post). In addition, at the two year follow up, the results stayed the same without any further issues or lapsing back into depressive states. This study proved that alpha and beta brainwaves actually got rid of depression in the brain. The most amazing thing is that meditation actually creates alpha and beta brainwaves and can assist in getting rid of any and many depressive states in the mind.

Meditation also solves the psychology of depression. Depression is deep within the brainwaves, and meditation actually breaks up these cycles and allows the brain to explore and go within and explore other arenas and allows it to circulate by its own means. It also gets rid of the regular depressive thoughts. People with depression often tend to have a chemical imbalance going on which forces them to feel low, sad, and depressed. As a result, they often have thoughts of "I'm not good enough, I'm not wanted etc," and the great thing is that meditation actually has the ability to rid a person of these unwanted unhealthy thought patterns.

Meditation also opens the door to a higher consciousness and a very advanced mental awareness. A person then has the ability to remain calm and well-balanced rather than going into states of being too low or too high. Meditation can actually result in a brain that is hardwired to fight depression and stay extremely health and well-balanced.

It allows you to gain a spiritual wholeness so that you don't have an empty void which can lead to depression and depressive thoughts. Meditation also exterminates depression completely from the brain and allows a greater amount of neurotransmitters to be present which actually fills the brain with neurotransmitters and gets rid of depression very quickly. With meditation, you can actually boost serotonin to healthy depression resistant levels in a very natural form. Meditation creates a neuro chemical arena where depression literally is unable to survive in the brain cells. Meditation also deactivates the anxiety and depression centers of the brain.

Other natural ways to beat and heal depression and become a happier and more positive person include: Exercise, sleep, herbal medicine, alternative healings, nature and the outdoors, Healthier diet, yoga, b vitamins, music, acupuncture, massage, and dietary supplements, avoid alcohol and drugs, relaxation, guided imagery, **5-Hydroxytryptophan (5-HTP). 5-HTP** is a naturally occurring chemical. It works by increasing the amount of serotonin in the brain. Serotonin is associated with mood, sleep, and other functions, and the increase of it can assist with depression. Kava is a root from the kava plant that's known for its sedative and anesthetic properties. It's most commonly used as an ingredient in relaxing teas. Kava's relaxing effects have been likened to benzodiazepines which can assist with depression due to easing tension and anxiety.

Eat a serotonin-enhancing diet. Many antidepressants like Prozac act by inhibiting the reuptake of serotonin by receptors in the brain, and increase serotonin levels. You can actually increase your brain's serotonin levels by eating foods that boost your serotonin levels naturally. Serotonin-enhancing foods are foods such as wild salmon, sardines, herring, mackerel, anchovies, healthy fats like coconut oil, and a high protein diet like free-range turkey. Avoid caffeine, which reduces serotonin levels, and expose yourself to sunlight which can increase Vitamin D.

Exercise can help release endorphins which can stimulate a rigid mind and assist with the chemicals and neurotransmitters in the brain. Getting enough sleep allows your body to exist in its own natural circadian rhythms and stay healthy, and being depressed can sometimes hinder this from happening. Herbal medicines like Lavendar and chamomile can have a host of positive natural effects similar to medications that can assist with depression or even other mental illnesses. Alternative healings can be anywhere from acupuncture to naturopathy and these healings can assist in helping with any form of depression or mental health issues. Massage can assist with releasing and helping with chemicals in the brain and can circulate the body and allow a person to feel less stress, and happier in general.

Chapter 9

Happiness and Morality:

Morals and happiness

Morality refers to a set of principles or values that guide individuals or societies in determining what is right or wrong, good, or bad, and how one ought to behave. It often involves concepts such as fairness, justice, empathy, and respect for others.

Morality is the governing principle that allows a person to develop their own belief systems, habits and ways of living and allows a person to understand the concepts in their territory that define the values between what is right and wrong. Morals are principles or beliefs that guide individuals in determining what is right or wrong, and they often do shape general behavior and decisions.

People tend to develop morals through a combination of upbringing, cultural and societal influences, personal experiences and their education usually. These aspects generally shape a person's beliefs, values and ethics over time.

Morals can often differ or vary across cultures due to variations in religious beliefs, social norms and tradition. Various cultures can basically have differing values which leads to differences in moral perspectives and behaviors. Happiness and morality are distinct concepts though they can be connected. Happiness refers to a subjective state of well-being and satisfaction, morality refers to the concept between right and wrong guiding ethical behavior. Acting morally can actually lead to long-term happiness and fulfillment as it aligns with one's values and promotes positive relationships and a sense of purpose. The relationship between happiness and morality can vary between cultures and societies.

In order to be a happy person, you will need to live by the golden rule. You can't just live your life doing what you want and living the way you like or doing what benefits you only. You will need to live by the rules and laws of goodness and nature.

How do morals relay into the concept of happiness- this makes no sense? Shouldn't I just do what makes me happy regardless of how it makes others feel?

Well, the answer to that is no of course. In order to truly be happy, we must live by the rules and laws of nature and the golden rules. To do unto others what you want done to you and to do unto each and every living being that which is moral and just is a concept that is lost in today's world and society. People often tend to do things which serves them only, and which will benefit them only and not which benefits humanity as a whole.

In order to be happy and live by the rules of happiness you will need to abide by all the laws of nature which are the laws of the universe and of humanity. You will need to live your life as a moral decent upstanding living creation that only does that which is beneficial to others and helpful and nothing that which is hurtful. For to hurt any living creation goes against all karmic rules and laws and goes against the laws of nature love and life.

People tend to do that which benefits them usually. It's usually not a decent scenario where someone is thinking of others and how to be a moral and good person when they commit actions in this world and do specific deeds. People typically will tend to do things that serve them and not that which serves humanity as a whole. In order to achieve true happiness, you'll need to live your life by serving humanity and doing the best of deeds, and only then can you truly be a happy and good person and live with a clear conscience and live in the manner of goodness decency and humbleness. The true way to happiness is morality and living by the golden rule of goodness and being an upstanding amazing human being and being proud of who you are deep within.

Being an upstanding amazing human being is one of the few ways of achieving true happiness and it is the way to achieving happiness and the path to true happiness. Once you're living by the golden rules of life karma and the laws of nature and the universe, you can truly be a happy good person and truly love yourself and love each and every aspect of you and others as well. This is one of the few ways of achieving the beauty and concept of happiness and goodness and being at one with yourself and living the life you were meant to live and the life you've always dreamed of.

The key to being a good person is true happiness and the concept of morality that truly encompasses doing good deeds and possessing the culpability of being a happy and positive great person who lives his or her life by the golden rule of goodness and morality.

Happiness and morality go hand in hand because in order to truly be happy and a good person you need to be engulfed in doing good deeds and being a moral person. Of course, you can be happy without following a moral code, but this is just the better more effective and right thing to do over doing whatever you feel suits you best. Selflessness is the key to a moral lifestyle and upbringing and it's really important to understand that in order to be a truly happy positive person you'll need to abide by a decent moral law or code of some form.

We need to be and live that which we seek out of others. It's important to live and be and practice beauty and positivity and abstain from doing harmful or negative deeds. We are the most important creatures in our universe, and we are in fact the creators of our universe and everything that occurs in it.

Morality is the key to being a better person and a happier livelier one. We can't just sit back and think that things are going to get better for us or that our lives will magically just improve on their own. We need to focus on being better people and doing good deeds, and that is to build on positive energy and goodness and allow this positivity to harness and work through and let us be better humans and people in general and improve and be happier as we are.

There are several steps and means that a person can increase or make greater their levels of morality or their true moral nature. It's a good thing to try to strive to be a more moral or exemplary person in general. It not only will affect your self-esteem and your life in general, it will boost your happiness and allow you to be a more fulfilled human being who is proud of the beliefs and principles that you stand for.

Increasing morality involves conscious effort and self-reflection. Some ways to enhance morality include:

1. Educate yourself: Learn about ethical principles, moral philosophies, and different perspectives to broaden your understanding of life, education, culture and history.
2. Practice empathy: Cultivate empathy by putting yourself in others' shoes and considering their perspectives and feelings.
3. Reflect on values: Regularly reflect on your values and how they align with your actions. Identify areas for improvement and set goals to act in accordance with your moral compass.
4. Seek moral role models: Look up to individuals who exemplify moral behavior and learn from their actions and choices.
5. Engage in moral discussions: Participate in discussions and debates about moral issues to deepen your understanding and challenge your own beliefs.
6. Act with integrity: Make a conscious effort to act in line with your moral principles, even when it may be challenging or inconvenient.

7. Practice self-awareness: Develop self-awareness to recognize and manage biases, prejudices, and unethical tendencies.
8. Reflect on consequences: Consider the potential impact of your actions on others and society as a whole.
9. Cultivate moral courage: Stand up for what you believe is right, even in the face of opposition or adversity.
10. Seek feedback: Be open to feedback from others and use it as an opportunity for growth and self-improvement.

Remember, morality is a lifelong journey, and it's important to continuously strive to be a better person for this will allow you to become a happier more fulfilled person overall as well.

Chapter 10

How To Boost Your Happiness

Happiness is a state of mind and a place that you'll need to find once you reach the levels of ecstasy and goodness that you need to be at in order to be a happy person. You can also boost your happiness in many different ways. You have access to happiness at any given time and don't have to do much in order to get to it.

The happier you are and the place and person that you were always meant to be but that person that has been extremely difficult to reach or attain. There are many ways a person can boost their happiness and become more positive enriched human beings and live more fulfilling lives. The true happiness you seek, is something that you'll always find if you're searching deep enough and wanting to know more about yourself and all the amazing things and qualities that you possess.

Happiness is the beauty we were all meant to and blessed to be with and how we were truly blessed to live with. To be a happy and healthy person is the ultimate nirvana and many people's dreams and goal in life. Imagine, if you can achieve this for yourself, then how would you feel overall as a person? Would you feel as if everything in your life would just come together, or would you feel as if there was more you could do to be a better person overall and allow your life to become more fulfilled? Is happiness really the key for you to living a grand and gracious effervescent existence? If so, then you definitely don't have to worry about things being worse than they are for you and you're lucky to be on such a unique wavelength of thinking for once you finally attain the happiness and goodness you so deserve and desire, then everything else in life will seem much easier for you and any hardships or issues can easily go away with ease as compared to the way things were before!

Happiness is not an easy state to achieve it can be extremely difficult, and it takes effort, sometimes in order to reach height and sense of happiness, or excitement, or even an elevated sense of happiness especially if you're in a place where you don't possess those feelings.

Have you ever wondered why some people seem extremely happy while you seem very sad. Well, the problem is that those people who seem extremely happy might not be happy or living happy fulfilled lives. They may also be living in a total lack of awareness and might just seem as if they're happy on the surface. I'm sure you've heard of how people are generally not as happy as they seem to be on the surface. Once again, most people live in states of shallowness and lack of awareness. While they may seem extremely happy and living a carefree existence on the surface, they don't truly possess those feelings on the inside or lack the awareness within to truly be happy people.

You might be extremely confused and wonder why some people just seem happier than others. Shelly, a 25-year-old coworker of yours always seems happy, and it always has a smile on her face however, you have no idea how she truly feels on the inside or where her happiness stems from. It's extremely difficult to find people that possess genuine happiness out there. She seems very happy and as if everything is going great for her most of the time, however, the plain truth is, you have no idea how she truly feels inside or what kind of issues ail her on a daily basis. You may feel as if you're the only one with major issues within yourself, but rest assured, you're definitely not the only one out there who feels this way.

On the other hand to her, you might seem the exact same kind of person, maybe deep down within yourself you're not as happy, but on the outside, you seem extremely happy the truth is that there are many ways to achieve happiness, and to be a happier and better you And those ways can be achieved by extreme positive thinking, and by changing your mindset by changing your life in a hugely positive way.

To be a positive magnet and someone who lives and bathes in positivity, you'll need to really focus on the concept of love and goodness in anything that you do. We are all positive beings and people somewhere deep within ourselves, but those wonderful elements of ourselves tend to have gotten lost in the general phase of who we are and in our daily lives. We often tend to forget what it means to be positive and how to live like this on a daily basis and how to be and exist within a positive realm of life.

There are major amounts of greed and confusion that have taken over us, so the question is, how on earth can be become powerhouses of positivity and allow this to radiate within us and let us be that which we once were or who we were meant to be?

We basically just need to think on a much higher plane and focus on being part of a higher mode of thinking, rather than thinking in lower levels which are greed, selfishness, lack of awareness etc. We need to engulf ourselves with positive statements in life and positive affirmations throughout various moments of our day, and then build upon those moments in order to focus on being a positive powerhouse.

Does it seem like others just seem happier than you are? Do you often look to others and think "he or she just seems as if they are happier people living greater and more fulfilled lives?" Well the truth is, you seem the exact same way to them or to many others out there!

Do fun-filled positive enlightening activities

I'm sure you've heard of the statement, you are what you do, not what you'll say you do.

So it's really important that you fill your life and days with fun-filled positive activities for these things will allow you to become a more positive, happier person and fill your life with happiness and good ideations and grand beneficial experiences over negatives ones.

Theme parks and amusement parks are a great way to fill your day or your experiences with positivity and light and excitement.

Theme parks aren't as boring or plain as they seem to be or even cheesy. They are actually a wonderful and gracious place for a person to engulf in self-care, love and goodness and they're packed with happy families on vacation just looking to have a good time. Theme parks are full of amazement, wonder, joy and the positivity you'll need to have a grand old time and raise your elements and vibration and become a happier and better person.

Group events with friends or co-workers are also a great way for you to fill your days and life with positive fun-filled experiences. There is a website called 'meetup.com', where you'll be able to find like-minded people who enjoy going to groups and doing group activities and you'll find that they have a great time together and enjoy being positive most of the time.

Religious temples are an excellent way for you to embrace and engulf positive aspects of life and for you to gain greater spiritual insight into your life and within your realm and world of experiences. There are various religions where you can find religious temples where you're able to do this including Hindu temples, Buddhist temples, Islamic mosques, and Christian churches. Each place of worship can give you unlimited access to learning and to various ways of improving your life and also give you insight on how to live life and moral codes to live by as well. They usually have religious and spiritual teachings at these places of worship including satsangs, sermons, and khutbahs, and you can learn a variety of important things from going to these places and boost your spirituality, positivity and become a happier more whole person. Going to these places helps increase your spiritual levels as well which can help you become a happier person and rid you of any negative ideas or vibes you may have.

Take up positive activities- go to a movie, play mini- golf. Movies are a great way of relaxing a person and creating a host of positive energy and allow a person to become immersed in their own selves and their own goodness and positive emotions. Therapists often recommend movies to help change the way we think or feel. Therapists prescribe movies to help their patients explore their psyches. Movies are becoming one more tool to help those in therapy achieve their goals and achieve more positive results in life and help boost good and positive emotions.

Take a cruise or go on vacation. Taking a vacation can help boost and build up positive emotions and vibes and help you be a happier person overall.

Go to the beach or on a boat- water can be a great healer and can be of wonderful benefit to a person. It can eradicate negative emotions and vibrations and create wonderful beautiful positive vibes and allow a person to become a healthier and happier person overall

Get a massage- you definitely need one. Your internal make up is full of all kinds of pent up tension, and negative emotions. It can help release negative energies and allow the body to heal.

Therapy and support is an excellent way of healing and helping oneself and even creating various positive energies. Therapy can be a great healing modality and can generate positive energies and can help you heal from any issues or trauma and allow you to become a happier person.

Surround yourself with positive people. It is very important to surround yourself with a positive support system and positive people and those who will assist you and cheer you on and good healthy people. It's extremely important to do this in order to further help you embrace your own strengths and great qualities and improve your overall life.

Chapter 11

Workbook Section and Journaling

In this section, you'll want to workbook and journal your experiences and life in order to better improve your state of mind and become one and more whole with yourself, and improve your life, your state of mind, and your self-esteem.

1. Write out a list of positives and negatives about yourself and your life
2. Write out a list of things you are thankful, grateful and blessed for in your current life

   Look over this journal and experience on a daily basis and keep adding to it daily in order to increase your blessings. Be sure to be very grateful and happy for all the wonderful blessings you do have and the ones you add to as well.

3. After writing out #1, you'll need to add more positives to it and keep writing out many different positive things that you feel about the positives and build on those things.
4. Try to eradicate the negatives out. For instance, focus on the positives and keep writing more and more positive aspects of the positive aspect of your life- build on that positivity. Slowly erase the negative aspects that you wrote down
5. Reread everything that you have written, let it absorb and soak into you and allow your brain and mind to immerse those positive beliefs or aspects into your mind and your subconscious mind. Do this daily, and watch the results- you will begin to focus more on the positive and beautiful and good aspects of your life rather than the negative.

6. Try to eliminate and eradicate all the negative aspects of your life or ways you feel negative about yourself. Write out all the negative aspects of your life on a piece of paper and either burn it or throw it away, leaving only the positive aspects of yourself there.
7. Write out a list of positive and negative emotions you have throughout the day.
8. Focus on the positive emotions, and think about how you can eradicate those negative emotions that might take over you or drain you throughout your days and your personal experiences.
9. Write out a list of positive affirmations that best describe you such as "I am special, I am attractive, I am a fun person." Each and everyday, add to these affirmations.

   Write out more and more affirmations and very soon you'll have a powerhouse list of positive affirmations that you've created yourself that you can use to help boost your self-esteem and your state of mind. Repeat these affirmations daily, and use them to build your sense of self-worth, your current inner positivity, and allow them to change the state of your mind.
10. Begin to journal your emotions and experiences and have a separate section of negative and positive experiences

that you had throughout the day. Focus on the positive experiences you had throughout the day and what you'll want to do with the negative experiences is replace them with positive thoughts, and rewrite the story to where it turned into a positive experience. This will slowly allow you to replace those negative events and thoughts into more positive, helpful and beneficial ones.

For Example:

Positives	Negatives
I am a fun person (I am beautiful, bubbly, interesting)	sometimes I get down on myself
I am good company for others (I'm fun, positive, outgoing often) (im kind hearted, carefree)	I get moody often easily
I like to do nice things for people	

It's extremely important to write out as many positives as you can about the good things that do make up the wonderful person that you are. You'll want to focus on those positive aspects of yourself and build upon them. It's extremely important that you do this on a regular basis daily and remind yourself of all the great positive things that you do possess and that you can build upon.

It's also important to slowly erase all the negatives or cross them out and focus only on the positive qualities that you do hold for yourself. You'll want to focus only on the positives for this is what will allow you to build on your goodness and help you become a whole and happier person overall.

Hopefully this book helped you understand the many concepts of happiness and the different ideas regarding being a happier and more positive person. Being a positive person is a very important task to undergo. You will hopefully end up achieving the many and great successes you deserve and live a happy and fulfilling life.

www.ingramcontent.com/pod-product-compliance
Lightning Source LLC
LaVergne TN
LVHW012026060526
838201LV00061B/4488